Fisher of Men
at Glasgow Docks

Sam Laughlin

JOHN RITCHIE LTD
CHRISTIAN PUBLICATIONS

40 Beansburn, Kilmarnock, Scotland

ISBN-13: 978 1 907731 75 4

Copyright © 2012 by John Ritchie Ltd.
40 Beansburn, Kilmarnock, Scotland

www.ritchiechristianmedia.co.uk

Typeset by John Ritchie Ltd., Kilmarnock
Printed by Bell & Bain Ltd., Glasgow

Contents

A collection of short stories of one man's Christian Crusade among the Seamen who came in to Glasgow Docks 1990-2007

Dedication

This book is dedicated to my wife, Wilma, with love,
and to the friends at Bethesda Hall, Linthouse, Glasgow
for all their Christian love, interest, and support
during the many years I worked for the Lord
among the seamen at King George V Docks, Glasgow.

Credits

Many thanks are due to Graeme Hewitson,
Artist and Graphic Designer,
for the beautiful and evocative book cover
and for the excellent freehand drawings
of ships' memorabilia throughout the book.

Many thanks also to Alan Cameron and Douglas Kennedy
for their expert work on the production of the book.

The Old Gospel Hall

There are buildings in Glasgow of worldly renown,
They soar to the sky like icons of stone.
They're lovely to look at; their history is grand,
Well admired for their beauty as proudly they stand.

There's the Burrell, the Mitchell, and Kelvingrove too,
And wonderful buildings the folk love to view.
The tourists all flock from Japan and from Spain,
To see these fine buildings and what they contain.

There's a building in Linthouse (though it's rather small),
It's near to the river where ships often call.
Away tucked between the tenements tall,
Is the place that is called "The Old Gospel Hall".

Its name is "Bethesda", a good Bible name,
Like many who gather within its domain.
God in His love gave His Son for us all,
Who believe in His Word at the Old Gospel Hall.

There are locals who come, and strangers and all,
From Russia and China, and far off Bengal.
They hear the glad story ~ "Christ died for us all" ~
That's why it is there ~ The Old Gospel Hall.

It's not built of marble, there's only one floor,
With no fancy stonework surrounding the door.
But for one hundred years it has stood every squall,
This quaint little building – The Old Gospel Hall.

It's a place of sweet fellowship to remember the Lord,
And to sing songs of Zion and study God's Word.
For Christ has redeemed us once and for all,
O thanks be to God for The Old Gospel Hall.

Sam Laughlin - 2002

Foreword

Sam Laughlin is an evangelist – although he has never conducted a Gospel campaign and has rarely preached from a platform. This book, in a series of anecdotes, tells the story of Sam's years of bringing the Gospel, one-to-one, to seafarers from around the globe. He did this without ever leaving Glasgow. Sam grasped that God was bringing the world to his doorstep. He rose to the challenge and met it enthusiastically.

Sam Laughlin is a Glasgow man through and through. Although of Ulster stock he was born and bred near the docks in Kinning Park. He spent most of his working life in the Clyde shipyards. Not surprisingly his characteristically Glaswegian sense of humour comes through time and again in these stories.

Sam Laughlin has a genuine interest in people from all over the world. He is eager to learn about their background and culture. Best of all, he has an unmistakable concern for their physical and spiritual welfare. Sam treats everyone as a unique individual, precious in God's sight.

Sam Laughlin has a supportive life partner in his wife Wilma. Together they have sacrificially used their home for Christ, opening it to welcome strangers from many parts of the world. They opened their hearts too, keeping in touch with many of those visitors and their families. Theirs has been a team ministry.

Above all, Sam Laughlin loves the Lord Jesus and cherishes the Gospel. His confidence in the message of Amazing Grace and

Christ's power to save and keep is the foundation of the service described in this book. That confidence led him to commence it and encouraged him to continue it.

God's work today needs many more servants like Sam.

Alan J. Gamble

Fisher of Men at Glasgow Docks

Introduction

During my sixteen years of boarding the ships, hundreds of men - and women - attended our gospel service in Bethesda Hall on a Sunday evening and came afterwards to my home for supper. Did I have any fears? Well, we all have fears, but it was the Lord's work I was doing and I have always been aware that if I am in His service he equips me for the job in hand. Instead of fear, I knew great joy to hear them singing the old hymns and choruses as Wilma accompanied them on the keyboard in our home. I had all the familiar hymns and choruses ready printed out on large pieces of cardboard. Did they love to sing? Yes, they did! No matter what country they came from, they loved to sing! I got them to repeat each of the choruses at least three times so that they could learn the words and take back home with them something of the contents (remember these men were not native English speakers). I kept to the simple easy-to-sing hymns like *Jesus Loves Me This I Know* and

> *Will your anchor hold?*
> *In the storms of life,*
> *When the clouds unfold*
> *Their wings of strife?*
> *When the strong tides lift,*
> *And the cables strain,*
> *Will your anchor drift*
> *Or firm remain?*

On Christmas morning, I always got up early to visit the docks with bags of goodies hoping that there would be a few ships in dock. Driving through the districts of Ibrox and Govan and Linthouse on Christmas morning was like driving through an empty city – not a car or human being in sight. Although it was ten o'clock in the morning, many of the citizens would be having a long lie after staying up late the night before – Christmas always means "party time" in Scotland!

The ships that were in dock welcomed me with open arms. I gave each seaman a carrier bag containing Tunnock's Carmel Wafers, chocolate Wagon Wheels, Jaffa Cakes, and sweets, as well as a New Testament, a Christmas card, a hand-knitted woolly hat and a calendar! I also handed out Christian literature – in their own language if possible.

The stories in this book are for the glory and praise of God for all that has been done in His Name. It is my hope that people will be challenged, whether Christian or not, by what they read in this book. The last thing I want to do is give anyone the idea that I had a big impression of my own importance. The glory is the Lord's!

He Changed His Mind

It was lunch time as I approached the average-sized cargo ship. I reckoned there would be about ten or twelve of a crew on board. I usually look for a member of the crew before I board a ship - to find out their nationalities so that I can take calendars and New Testaments in appropriate languages on board with me. On this occasion, no crew member was visible on deck but I saw a docker coming down the gangway. I asked him where the crew came from and he said "From Poland".

I hurried back to my car to load my bag with Polish literature. As the local docker walked alongside me, I asked him if he would like a Christian calendar. He said, rather grudgingly, that he did not mind, so I gave him a couple for the New Year!

I returned to the ship but, as it was lunch time, there was nobody around. I soon found the mess room, however, where there was a good number of seamen present. I introduced myself and laid out my literature on one of the tables. I told them to take anything they wanted. "All free," I said. "No money."

Soon there was a curious crowd of seamen around the table. Observing their interest, I said "Take some for yourselves - and your friends at home as well."

Suddenly a tall, rough-looking, man appeared in the doorway. He glared at me and shouted angrily, "Who you? We not want you! You go!" Moving to the table containing the literature he swept his hands to and fro across the table until every piece of literature was scattered on the floor – watched by the clearly embarrassed crew.

I said nothing but stood my ground – and then bent down and gathered up all the leaflets and books and placed them back on the table. By this time, the culprit had left the room – still shouting. I smiled and said to the crew "Very nice gentleman!" Soon, lunch-time was over and the crew left the mess room and returned to their duties – taking with them a good share of the literature! I stood staring through the porthole that looked out on the deck thinking about the angry man "What was he up to? Why was he in such a rage?" Suddenly I noticed him walking along the deck, but he hesitated as he came to the porthole and glanced in at the mess room. He was up to something! Why was he glancing in at the porthole? I decided to shift my stance away from the porthole…and waited. What would he do? Was he waiting until the crew were all gone from the mess room – and then perhaps attack me?

I stood well back and kept my eye on the porthole as well as the door and watched. After a few minutes, there he was again – glancing in as he walked past in the opposite direction! I moved a bit further away and stood looking at a picture on the wall with my back to the door but making sure I could see the door reflected in the glass. I thought about his impulsive action in brushing my literature from the table. Why had he come back again? He was up to something – but what was it? My literature was still lying on the table. Should I pack up and leave? But I waited…after five minutes I sensed a movement at the door and watched the handle turn and the door slowly open. It was the big man himself. He was on tip-toe, moving towards the table and completely ignoring me. Would he scatter my books again? Would he throw them into the river - and maybe me as well? But no . . . . . he stretched out his hand and quietly picked up a calendar from the table; he then picked up a New Testament and, glancing up furtively, he made for the door. I turned slowly and said "Hello!" in a loud voice. He stopped, turned round, and looked at me. I walked towards him and stretched out my right arm. He gripped my hand and we shook hands. He never said a word. I said "God bless you!" – and he hurried off down the passage with his calendar and New Testament in his hand. I never saw him again.

I gathered up what remained of my literature, zipped up my bag, and left for another ship.

Just Pray About It

It was an American ship – painted a gleaming white. It looked new - not a mark on it as it shone in the morning sunshine. The man on security at the top of the gangway was a nice black man. I told him who I was and he welcomed me aboard and asked me to sign the visitors' book. When he checked what I had written he said, "Your name is Sam? I am Sam too!" We laughed and I said "Just call me Mr. Sam and I will call you Mr. Sam!" He liked that idea and laughed out loud. I gave him a knitted hat and said, "Mr. Sam, will you take me to the mess room?"

Just then, an officer appeared and offered to take me to the mess room himself. On the way, he said he was the Supply Officer. "My name is John," he said, and it was clear that he was very proud of his ship. He would say "Is this the best ship you have ever seen?" and would pause and run his hand over the bulkhead. "Look at this, Mr. Sam – beautiful! And, you know, this ship is guided by satellite navigation." Going through the galley, he stopped at the huge butcher's block. "Wow!" I said. "It must weigh at least a ton!" "No, Mr. Sam, I think nearer two tons – they can butcher a whole cow on that block!" "Wow!" I thought. "A whole cow!"

As we entered the Ship's Lounge, his pace quickened. "Look at this ice cream machine, Mr. Sam – 20 different flavours. Come along, I will show you the soda fountain and the coca-cola machine! And what about coffee? We have many different brands." "I would love a coffee," I said. "Black will be fine."

John asked me what I worked at. I told him I had been a ship's carpenter and had helped build ships. "Big ships?" he asked. "Biggest in the world," I said. "The Queen Mary, the QE2, and the Royal Yacht Britannia – but your ship is the most beautiful small ship I have ever been on!"

John now reckoned that it was time to change the subject and begin on his life story. He was fifty, he said, and not married yet, but there was a lady back home that was pushing him. She was 37, rich, and drove a big car. She was a singer, John said. "Country & Western?" I asked him. He looked horrified. "Oh no – opera!" I asked him what the problem was. He was fussy, he said, as far as a wife was concerned. She was well off and he was a seaman without much money. "Well," I said, "if you were a Christian I would tell you to pray about it." "I am a Christian," he said. "Well, John," I confided, "I hope she is a Christian, but if she is not a Christian you are richer than she is." "Yes, you are right, Mr. Sam. I've got Jesus Christ as my Saviour and my home in Heaven. But I do like the big car." I shook his hand and said again "Just pray about it."

Later, as I stood at the top of the gangway on my way home, Samuel the security man said, "Have a good day, Mr. Sam!" Remembering our pact on my arrival at the ship, I replied, "God bless you, Mr. Sam!" which made him laugh again. John appeared, shook my hand, and whispered "I will take it to the Lord in prayer."

As I drove off, I pumped the horn and they waved until I was out of sight. I never saw John again, but I hope he always will take his problems to the Lord in prayer.

Lana

It was an all-Russian crew of twenty-one men and one woman. She was a poor hard-working soul from Murmansk in the far north-west of Russia. She worked in the kitchen and the galley and the mess room of the ship, from 5.00 a.m. until 7.00 p.m. serving up meals, clearing and cleaning the tables, washing up dishes and pans. She was a small woman about thirty years old – with never a minute to call her own.

She could speak a little English and over-heard me giving out the invitation to come to Church. She said she would like to come. "I come with you" she kept saying. "All right, I said, "be ready at 6 o'clock." "But, she said "I work until 7 'clock, but please wait." "O.K.," I said, "but hurry!" And I sat down to wait while she hurried. I was really sorry for her and had not the heart to leave her behind. The gospel meeting at our church begins at 6.30 and it was already 6.15. When the time reached 6.30 I said "I must go." She pleaded, "Wait, wait!" and she scrubbed and cleaned and washed pots and swept floors until about 6.45 she said "Ready!"

Whether she had any other clothes or not, or did not have time to change, I do not know, but she did not put on anything else but came as she was – slippers, no stockings, a thin skirt and a light blouse and jacket. When we got to the Church, which is about two kilometres from the docks, we were already half an hour late – so we slipped in to a seat at the back. At the end of the service I introduced her to my wife and several others: "This is Lana from Russia!" Then she came home with Wilma and me for supper. I had had a good lot of ladies clothes given to me for those in need of them – and she fitted the bill. Wilma rigged her out with a blue anorak and shoes and cardigan – and also gave her other useful clothing for cold weather. She was delighted with it all, and after supper we played the keyboard and sang some choruses. I took her back to the ship and she was very happy. I helped her up the gangway with her bags of clothes and a Russian language New Testament and Christian calendar and Seed Sowers' text. I was not sure if she could read English well, but I said "You read; good read!" The ship sailed away the next day and we never saw Lana again but we hope she remembers her happy Sunday in Glasgow at The Old Gospel Hall.

Judy's Rescue Mission

The American catamaran-type ships which came in to Glasgow quite regularly had a crew of about 30 – a mixture of Ordinary Seamen and regular navy men. They were a sort of spy ship of a type used during the cold war with the USSR from about 1970-1990. One Captain took me on a tour round one of the ships and told me that if a Russian ship moved from a port in Russia, it could be tracked down; if it moved out of the dock in Murmansk, for instance, in Northern Russia, the American ship could follow its every move – such was the sophistication of the American ship's satellite navigation.

Another thing I noticed on this type of American ship: they always seemed to have a female or two aboard! One day I met a tall lady who was visiting the ship, and I invited her to the gospel service. Judy told me she was a born-again Christian and agreed to come along on the following Sunday, bringing her seaman husband, Jim, with her. She said she was not a member of the crew but she had received permission to come over for four days to be with Jim in Glasgow.

She was a very nice lady but she seemed worried. I duly picked Judy and Jim up from the ship on the Sunday and we went to our church, after which they came to our house for supper. Jim seemed a nice quiet man and we had a happy evening. Before returning to the ship after supper, Judy said she would like to visit us again - so, on the following Tuesday before she left for the airport for the journey back to New York, Judy arrived at our house by taxi. She was wearing a beautiful black scarf, with "Jesus Saves" printed on it in gold lettering – and had little presents for both of us. During lunch, she told us she was glad to have had the opportunity to be with Jim and valued the time they had spent together. Life is often hard for the wife of a seaman when her husband is far away. Judy had been anxious about Jim and that was why she came all the way to Scotland to see him.

When Judy returned home to America she wrote to us thanking us for the time we spent together.

A short time later, the ship left Glasgow and I never heard from Jim and Judy again.

Life at sea is fraught with difficulties – especially in married life, where couples are separated for long periods and encounter many temptations along the way.

I met many Christian seamen during my visits to the ships and always tried to encourage them to hold fast in the storms of life.

M/V Bright Water

Nowadays, when some ships come in to the docks with a large cargo, the dockers work all night unloading the ship. This actually saves the ship owners' money, for the quick turn-round of the ship saves a few days' docking dues and water dues. Gone are the days when ships were in dock for up to two weeks and the seamen went gallivanting in every port. Crews are now cut to a minimum. Sometimes the crews do not know where they are. They ask me "What port is this? What country are we in?" There is nothing romantic about a seaman's life nowadays. The old saying of "a girl in every port" is not true any more.

I was on an Indian ship recently. There was a large notice at the top of the gangway: *No crew member to leave ship while in port.* No doubt this was to forestall anyone thinking of jumping ship. There was a man on guard at the top of the gangway armed with a baseball bat. He was a big stout man. Thinking he was an officer of the ship or the bosun, I said to him "What country do you come from?" He replied, "I'm fae Govan. Whit dae ye want to know fur?"

I eyed the baseball bat and said, "It's O.K. I just wondered!" After a moment I asked: "Is it all right if I go to the mess room to meet the crew? I am the Port Missionary." What's that?" he asked. I tried to explain who I was. "Well," he said, "I was no' tae let anyone aff, but they never said anything aboot lettin' anyone on! I'll let you on but you might no' get aff again!" At that moment, a ship's officer appeared with a lady friend, both making for the gangway – so, taking the opportunity, the security man pointed to my hard hat on which was printed the words "Port Missionary". Glancing at my hat, the officer said, "It's all right, he's a visitor."

I was taken to the mess room and soon was giving out knitted woolly hats and Christian literature. There were two Indian Christians among the crew from Kerala in South India, and also some from Goa. I spoke to them about coming to Church on Sunday but they told me that the ship would be away by then. In a way I was quite relieved about this because I would not have liked to explain to the stout security man how to get the crew off the ship and back on again!

I was in the mess room for about half an hour and it was time to leave. The stout security man was still on duty. "Aye," he said, "you're the mystery man!" "No," I said, "I'm the missionary man!"

And he waved me off with the words "Oh aye. O.K. pal. Cheers!"

M/V Oosterport

I was a bit late getting on to this ship, it being ten past six on a Sunday evening. The crew were all Russians. When I got to the Mess Room they were at their dinner. They welcomed me and asked me to join them for dinner! I told them I hadn't time as our church meeting began at 6.30 p.m. I gave them calendars in the Russian language and hats and other literature and invited them to the Gospel Meeting. Three of them got ready right away and we made for the car. We got to the church as they were singing the first hymn. Robert Revie, a good preacher from Ayrshire, was the speaker. He spoke about Paul at Athens.

After church, they came to our house for supper – and we all had a grand time singing choruses and hymns (one man was a very good singer). I taught them the chorus "I have decided to follow Jesus". Our friends, George and Margaret Courtney, were with us. One of the men was the ship's Captain. A young officer gave my wife, Wilma, a gift: a small mother-of-pearl box containing a string of rosary beads!

Captain Genova

For the first time ever, I took a telephone call on my land-line at home from a ship at sea! The ship was on the Irish Sea on its way to Glasgow. The Captain of the ship spoke to me – his name was Captain Genova. He said his ship would be calling in at Glasgow on the following day and he would like the chance to speak to me. He had recently taken over this particular ship and had found one of my visiting cards in the Captain's cabin.

I was waiting at Glasgow docks the next day when his ship arrived. When it berthed, I climbed the gangway and the seaman on watch took me to the Captain's cabin. The Captain was a young man of about 35 years of age. The crew were all Filipinos. He told me that when he had found my visiting card he saw on it the Bible verse from Psalm 107: 23-24.

> "They that go down to the sea in ships,
>   that do business in great waters,
>   these see the works of the Lord,
>   and his wonders in the deep."

He noted my name and telephone number and decided to get in touch with me. He told me that it was his intention to set up an evangelical church in the Philippines after he retired. Could I help him to collect some King James Authorised Version Bibles to use in his church?

I soon "spread the word" around my friends, asking for surplus Bibles, no matter how old, for this good cause. Over the next two years, whenever Captain Genova's ship called in to Glasgow, I supplied him with a good number of Bibles. He wanted all of the congregation to be reading the same version of the Bible, so it was the King James Authorised Version he requested. He himself had been brought up on the AV and always quoted from it.

One day I told him I had a very large pulpit Bible at home which had been given to me by an elderly neighbour many years ago. Would he be interested in taking this, I asked? It was a beautiful Bible – a work of art, with leather covers beautifully tooled and sculptured, and in perfect condition. When he heard about this Bible, he was delighted to accept, even without seeing it. When I arrived at the ship with the Bible I got two of the crew to carry it aboard; it weighed about a ton – well, nearly! The Captain declared that he had never seen a Bible like this in his life!

Sometime later, once his evangelical church had been established, Captain Genova wrote to me from Manila to say that the Bible had become a great attraction. I was glad to know that people were drawn to the Word of God as an object of beauty; I hoped they may also be drawn to read it too and believe it. I was glad, too, that I had found a "home" for this large Bible as I had kept it safely for many years hoping that it would eventually be put to good use.

I also gave Captain Genova Bible Concordances and Commentaries (which had been given to me by a Christian man in my church for just such a purpose) together with 100 Seed Sowers' texts and a quantity of Emmaus Bible Courses.

I had recently received a quantity of new Bibles free of charge from the Bible Spreading Union, a Christian organisation committed to spread the Word of God throughout the world – so I gave Captain Genova a few brand new Bibles too!

The Bible Spreading Union is just one of the several Christian organisations who have very generously supplied me with Christian literature. All literature was sent to me free of charge.

Money was never mentioned. Other Christian Organisations, eg., Trinitarian Bible Society and Emmaus Bible School and No Frontiers - all gave me generous discounts and other helps. (However, when I mentioned this to my assembly, they sent a generous gift every year.)

"Quisling"

One cold, dark and windy winter's night when I drove into King George V Dock, I saw a fair-sized Norwegian ship. I had seen the ship on previous visits and knew it came in regularly, carrying a cargo of cement. It was the only ship sitting at the top of the basin. I parked my car and moved towards the gangway to investigate. There was a big man on watch. I asked him where he came from and he said "Bulgaria". I enquired if it was all right to come on board and he nodded his head. I went back to the car for my bag and brought with me a parcel of clothes, including a lovely anorak. He pointed me in the direction of the mess room and turned back towards the gangway. Before continuing on my way, I gave him a woolly hat, a calendar and a Seed Sower's text, and the anorak I was carrying. He deserved them all for being on a four-hour watch on such a terrible stormy night.

In the mess room eight men sat at tables. One man got up – a tall man with a bald head – and shook hands with me. He introduced me to the others. He was the Captain of the ship and spoke very good English. He and another member of the crew were Norwegians and there was also one Russian, one Pole, two Lithuanians, and a couple of Bulgarians. I gave each of them a calendar and a hand-knitted woolly hat, and invited them to help themselves to the free literature that I had spread on the table. The Russian man was happy to receive a Russian New Testament and other booklets and, in general, they all seemed happy to see me.

I told the Captain that I had visited Kristiansand in Norway a few years ago. He talked a lot about the war when Norway was occupied by the Germans in 1940. We discussed the book The Shetland Bus which told of the fishing boats that plied the dangerous waters between Shetland and Norway throughout the war, carrying secret agents and arms. We talked of Leif Larsen, a great hero of Norway, who came to aid the British Army during the war - and also of Vidkun Quisling who was no hero. Quisling was an extreme nationalist leader in the Norwegian parliament who collaborated with Hitler. He had some support as a passionate patriot of his country - but his great mistake was that he believed that Germany would win the war. He secretly flew to Germany on more than one occasion and met Hitler to attempt to broker a deal for Norway. He told Hitler Norway would assist the Germans in exchange for a "good deal" after the war. But Quisling failed to win over the Norwegian people to his point of view. Returning to Norway from Germany close to the end of the war, he was apprehended by the Norwegian Resistance who, by now, had formed a government. Quisling got a fair trial, but was sentenced to death and executed by firing squad at Akershus Fortress in October 1945. Throughout the world ever after, the name "Quisling" became synonymous with the word "traitor".

The Norwegian Captain also spoke of the convoy of ships that took supplies to Russia, travelling up the coast of Norway and Finland to Murmansk. I recommended the book by Alistair McLean, HMS Ulysses, to him. The Captain fairly enjoyed the discussion but the other Norwegian, a young man, sat and stared blankly at me the whole time and never said a word. They gave me coffee and chocolates.

I wondered about the Christian situation in Norway and asked the crew to read the Christian literature I had given them. The Captain told me that Norway had a mainly Lutheran majority, but not many went to church. I told him that missionaries from our country, Nat and Jennifer Rodgers, have lived in Norway with their family for a number of years.

Rolland Divine Grace

It was a big ship, with a mixed crew comprising Russians, Ukrainians and Filipinos - and an Indian Captain. The cook came from Togo in Africa. They all wanted hand-knitted hats but I did not have enough to go round – when short of hand-knitted hats, I usually buy extra hats from a shop in Glasgow for £1.00 each. They are good hats and the seamen like them as well as the knitted ones. I do get a good supply of hand-knitted hats from various sources but there are not many knitters around nowadays.

In this ship, I came across a man from Africa with whom I got on well. He had a Christian background and, believe it or not, his name was Rolland Divine Grace.

When I was leaving the ship for the last time, he presented me with a large ornate porcelain elephant which he had bought in an African port. He printed my name on the under-side of the elephant's feet - "To Mr. Sam from Rolland Divine Grace".

I was interested in the name "Rolland Divine Grace". I congratulated him on having such a great name. I told him that John Newton, the famous sailor who got converted, wrote the famous hymn "Amazing Grace". I told him the meaning of divine grace – that it was the undeserved favour of God to us. I gave him a large framed Seed Sowers' text of John 3:16. On the reverse side, God's grace is explained.

He was very happy to hear all this. I still have his gift of the elephant prominently displayed in my home.

Russian Braveheart

A request came to me from Inverness in the North of Scotland asking me to visit a Russian seaman who had been seriously injured on board ship. He had overbalanced in stormy weather and fallen from the top deck of the ship to a lower deck and landed on his back on top of machinery. He was now in the Southern General Hospital in Glasgow, having been transferred there from Inverness as the Glasgow hospital had a specialist spinal unit.

I do not know how they had got my name and address but obviously someone in Inverness, who knew I visited the ships in Glasgow, had contacted the Inverness hospital and told them about me. Next day I visited Sergi in the Southern General Hospital Spinal Unit.

Sergi could speak only a little English but he seemed pleased to see me. He was in a bad way. His injuries were really serious. His spine and ribs and many bones were all shattered. He was lying on a bed specially made for those with spinal injuries. He could not move in the bed - and he was to have surgery very soon. He was quite a young man and, despite his injuries, he was very pleasant and remarkably cheerful.

Soon, he received extensive surgery but, unfortunately, he contracted an unknown hospital infection. I, for one, thought he would not survive. But he recovered and was soon back to his usual cheerful self. I continued to visit him on a regular basis and some of my friends from the church visited him too and brought him little presents. He had several operations and eventually he was given the sad news that he would never be able to walk again. As time went on he learned to speak better English and was able to communicate well. He was always cheerful and one day I congratulated him on his courage and good humour and he threw his right arm in the air (the one that could move) and said: "Me Russian – Russian man very brave!" He could not move in bed apart from his right arm. I told him stories from the Bible and read to him from the Daily Bread booklet. I told him to trust in Jesus for his future. I read to him from the Book of Revelation in the Bible. In Heaven the Bible tells us there will be no more sickness or pain, no tears or darkness. Revelation Chapter 21 says:

And God shall wipe all tears from their eyes
and there shall be no more death,
neither sorrow nor crying nor shall there be any more pain,
for the former things are passed away.

Sergi was glad when I told him this from the Bible.

After a couple of months they began to take him to the physiotherapy centre of the hospital in a wheelchair. To get him in to the wheelchair required a good deal of work. It required a "crane" mechanism which lifted him up out of the bed and then swung him out until he was above the wheelchair and then lowered him on to the chair. This involved great pain but he gritted his teeth and never complained. He got on very well with everyone. It was a joy to visit Sergi.

The ship he had been on was a factory fishing ship registered in Spain. When on furlough from the sea he lodged in Spain, and eventually bought a house in Spain - but he was slowly improving in hospital in Scotland and he was hoping he would be kept in Scotland as long as possible, for he appreciated that he was getting the best of treatment here. But I knew from past experience of sick foreign seamen that if the treatment was going to be long-term the time would come when he would be transferred to his own country for further treatment.

But the months passed and Sergi remained – until one day he told me they were sending him to a hospital in Spain. He was really sad about this but he realised that it was inevitable. He was getting free treatment here – which must have been costing the National Health Service a lot of money. So one day, when I arrived to visit him, his bed was empty. Shortly after this I got a letter from a hospital in Spain with a photograph of Sergi on an exercise machine. In the letter he thanked me for my help and told me how he missed all his friends in Glasgow. The letter, of course, was not written by him and the writer had not included Sergi's address. I thought of trying to contact every hospital in Spain to find out his whereabouts but I had no clue as to the city the letter had come from, or the hospital, or even his surname. We all just called him Sergi - but to me he was indeed a Russian Braveheart. It was a joy to have met with Sergi.

Sasha & Kufti

The large ocean-going tug had been lying-up for a number
of weeks. I had passed it a few times and it always seemed
deserted. It was in good order and not a rust-bucket by any
means. It was well-painted and tidy-looking but, somehow, I
never had any notion of trying to board it. Maybe it was in for
repairs, I thought.

Then one day I decided to take a look. There was a gangway
lying on the deck of the ship but I managed to climb aboard,
because the ship was almost level with the quay-side. It was a
risky business, climbing on board – one slip and I could have
fallen into the murky river beneath. I tried the doors on the open
deck and eventually found one I could open. This led down a
stair and into a long passage with cabin doors on either side.
There was no sound to be heard, or any sign of life. Near the end
of the passage, I noticed a door with a shaft of light shining out
from underneath. I stopped, not too sure what to do but, taking
courage, I knocked the door, turned the handle and walked into
the room! I found a man sitting at a desk, writing. "Hello!" I
said, as he looked up. He was a swarthy, stockily-built man. I
shook hands with him and left my bag on the floor. I explained
who I was and asked him where he came from. He told me he
was from Baku, the capital of Azerbaijan. The ship was for sale
and had recently been purchased by new Canadian owners. He
and another seaman were on board looking after the ship until
the handover. I asked him if the other man was on board but
he said he was not sure where he was – perhaps he had gone
into town. I displayed the books and other items I had in my
bag and he seemed interested. He took a Bible, a calendar, some

leaflets, and a woolly hat. He said his name was "Sasha". He asked me if I could bring him a newspaper if I came back. Kufti was the other seaman but I rarely saw him. Sasha was the one who remained on board to watch the ship. Before I left that day, I invited him to come to church on the following Sunday and then to my house for supper after the church service.

I called for him on Sunday at six o'clock, bringing with me the newspaper as promised, and found him in the same cabin - but he could not come with me until Kufti came back. He had told Kufti he was going out with me but so far there was no sign of him. We waited but by 6.30 p.m. (the time for church) he had still not returned. We waited for nearly an hour before Kufti arrived back at the ship – offering no apology for his late return. By this time my wife had arrived home from church and was up to high doh as I had not appeared at the evening service. She was about to phone the police when I arrived at our door with Sasha for supper.

Before we left to go back to the ship, I gave Sasha a plastic carrier bag with trousers and shirts and shoes. Around ten o'clock we arrived back at the ship. It was a dark and stormy evening and a strong wind was howling through the deserted dock. As we got out of the car, Sasha slung the bag over his shoulder and moved towards the gangway. He put out his hand and grabbed the rail of the gangway to haul himself aboard when the whole thing gave way and toppled sideways, throwing him to the ground and causing him to drop the bag of clothing into the river. Sasha tried to grab the bag, almost falling into the river as well. I was just behind him and if I hadn't taken a backward jump, I would have been in the river too.

The ship sailed away the following week, with a new crew, on its way to Chile and Sasha went home to Azerbaijan.

Sasha was a fine man and I hoped he would read the literature I had given him on my first visit to the ship and would trust in the Lord Jesus Christ for personal salvation.

Saturday Night Visit

It was a warm and sunny Saturday evening in May, and we were relaxing at home after our evening meal, when there was a knock at the door. Two men stood on the doorstep - one tall and one quite short. The tall one said: "Do you recognise me?" I looked at him keenly. "I'm afraid not," I said. He continued, "We are seamen from a ship docked on the River Clyde and I was a visitor to this house eleven years ago!" He told me his name was Ilya. Then my wife joined me and I asked her "Do you remember Ilya?" "Of course I do!" she replied. "Ilya from Ukraine? I write to his wife!" Then I remembered, and promptly invited both of them in for supper. He told me that the name of the ship they were on now was an Irish ship called "The Arklow Rally".

We enjoyed conversing with Ilya and hearing about his wife, Tanya, and his son, Peter. I asked him how he had managed to find my house. Eleven years is a long time, and on that occasion he had come to our house by car from church. It was amazing that he had been able to find our address again. He explained how he had done it. He and his fellow officer had decided to walk from the docks to our house and, with the aid of satellite navigation via mobile phone to guide the way, he was able to find our house five kilometres from the docks! Part of their journey was via the Clyde Tunnel footpath (their ship was based on the west side of the river) – a route under the River Clyde not much used and rather scary on a quiet evening! They had then emerged at the district of Govan, had walked through the district of Ibrox, and up past Bellahouston Park until they had arrived at our door. Ilya was now the Chief Officer of his present ship and his friend was the Engineer. We talked of old times and how his family in Ukraine have kept in touch with us throughout the years by correspondence and surprise gifts. He asked about our church and told how he had enjoyed his visit to it, and to our house afterwards for supper. We expressed the hope that some day soon he and his wife and son would come for a visit to Scotland.

I was not driving at this time, as I was recovering from a stroke, so the two men returned to their ship by taxi. As we parted, we all agreed that we had spent an enjoyable evening together. I gave him some Christian literature for his shipmates and family.

Sheila

It was February with a gale blowing and freezing cold as I boarded this small coaster from Dundalk in Ireland. There was five of a crew, all Irish. I gave them woolly hats and offered them literature but they were not too interested in that.

When I was leaving the ship to go down the gangway I encountered a young woman of about 18 painting the open deck. I spoke to her. She was a crew member from Dublin. Her name was Sheila and she was shivering in the cold wind that was blowing up the river. I gave her a knitted hat which she put on right away. I was sorry for her. She looked dejected. When I got to my car, I looked in the boot to see if I had any warm clothing I could give her but there was nothing suitable. Then I remembered the anorak I myself was wearing. I took it off and ran over to the ship, called her, and gave her the anorak and went back to my car and drove off.

I was happy I had been able to help someone in need. Was this not a Christian duty?

"When I was hungry you gave me meat, when I was thirsty you gave me drink. When I was a stranger, you took me in..." Jesus said. "Inasmuch as you have done it unto one of the least of these my brethren, you have done it unto me." Matthew 25:35.

Captain Reuben

The large ship in dock, with a Russian crew, was from Georgia – once part of the Soviet Union and now a separate country with its own government. Part of Turkey close to the border with Georgia once belonged to Georgia and wars over territory is part of Georgia's history, as it has been for many countries in that region. It was in that part of the world, on Mount Ararat, that Noah's Ark settled after the Flood.

When I reached the ship's mess room, I set out my Christian literature on a table and handed out warm hand-knitted woolly hats "All free!" I told the seamen as they crowded round – no money required!

They looked a rough lot but they welcomed me. Soon the Captain and Chief Engineer appeared in the mess room. The Captain said he wanted to speak to me as he was interested in Christian things. He was a fine, gracious man and we had coffee together in the mess room and then he invited me to his cabin.

He asked me for a Russian Bible and wondered if I could give him a video about Jesus. I returned the next day with the Russian Bible and the video "Who Is This Man, Jesus?" I invited Captain Reuben to our church service the following Sunday evening and he agreed to come.

On the Sunday, I picked him up in the car from the ship at six o'clock and when we got to the church I introduced him to the speaker, Brian Hill.

Captain Reuben was quite amused when I told him Brian's church was near Moscow in Ayrshire. He was even more amused when I told him that, some years ago, one of our well-known preachers was called Mr. Stallan and that he had no doubt preached at Brian's church near Moscow!

The Captain's name of Reuben caused me to think he may have had Jewish connections. He told me his daughter went to a house church in Georgia which preached about Jesus Christ. Captain Reuben enjoyed the gospel service in our church that night, and he gladly accepted the invitation to my home for supper afterwards.

I returned to the ship the following Tuesday and had a good conversation with Reuben. He told me there had been some difficulties on board. Many repairs were required before the ship left Glasgow.

I brought the crew some warm clothing as they looked very poor and ragged. They were very grateful for everything they got. I gave Captain Reuben a white leather covered New Testament to give to his daughter when he got home to Georgia.

The ship was delayed for a few more days in Glasgow but eventually they sailed for home. Even now, I still think and pray for my dear friend, Captain Reuben.

A Bird In The Wrong Bush!

Filipinos are by nature not very tall but they make up for their lack of inches in many other ways. They are cheerful, friendly, and happy, and like to meet strangers like me. Once they get to know you, they never forget you. And, of course, they all speak English, their second language after Tagalog, their native language.

On this particular ship, I met a very interesting Filipino. He was short in build – but full of energy. He came from one of the 7,000 inhabited islands that make up the Philippine Islands. He spoke almost perfect English and had perfect manners. But the most noticeable thing about him was that he had very bushy hair. His hair was cut to look like a rounded bush. I think he had it styled in this way to make him look taller.

I admired his hair and asked him how he managed to keep it so tidy. "Well, Mr. Sam," he said, "I never have it cut by the ship's barbers. They cut hair with a knife and fork! I have a real barber in Manila".

Then he told me of a rather unusual experience he had had one day when he was back home in the Philippines. It was a very hot sunny day and he thought he would lie down to rest for a while in a field not far from his home. Soon he fell into a deep sleep. Suddenly he had the feeling that someone was pulling his hair. He wakened in a panic, put his hand to his head, and found a large bird scrambling to free itself of his hair and fly off. He found stocks of grass in his hair where the bird had made a good start at building a nest!

All in all, I thought it was quite a hair-raising experience for him!

My Wounded Knee

In 2002 my left kneecap began to swell. I do not usually bother too much about things like that - but I wondered what was causing it. Some gangways are long and steep – which put a strain on one's knees; shorter gangways also could be dangerous if not securely fixed. Some ships had no gangway at all! I once climbed up the side of a ship on a rope ladder, swaying all over the place, and it was only by the grace of God that I landed safely on deck.

Maybe it was exploits such as those that caused my swollen knee. The time came when I could ignore it no longer and went to see my GP. A locum lady doctor saw me. She said she would arrange an appointment with the local hospital and, meantime, recommended pain killers. When I obtained my prescription from the chemist I discovered the pain killers were extra strong and about the size of a 50 pence piece! I checked the list of side effects, decided I would rather thole the pain in my knee, and threw the pain killers in the river.

While waiting for my hospital appointment to come up, I was using a walking stick and had a limp. One day I was limping across the quay-side towards a ship from Kiribati I had previously visited. As I approached the gangway a large rugby-type member of the crew hurried down the gangway towards me. "You have a bad leg, Mr. Sam" he shouted and gripped me in a bear-hug and carried me bodily up the gangway with my bag of literature and walking stick and planted me down on the deck of the ship, to much laughter from others of the crew who were looking on.

The story of my "wounded knee" has, however, a happy ending. In due course I was seen by the doctor at the hospital. He recommended "a little exploratory operation" but I managed to forestall this by asking for more time as, in the interval between my visit to my GP and my hospital appointment, my knee had felt better. The doctor gave me a new appointment for two months hence. When he saw me again, the swelling in my knee had disappeared and my knee was back to normal. When their ship returned to Glasgow, the Kiribati men were very happy to see me walking up the gangway with no sign of a limp!

A Saturday Night Tragedy

A seaman's life is a hard, demanding, and dangerous job, and the crew of a ship must all work together for their own protection. They often face perilous situations which require courage and determination and strength – such as mountainous seas and freak waves and great ocean swells. It is at times like these that a man needs to know that God is his anchor and Lord Jesus is his Saviour to enable him to withstand the storms of life.

Some thoughts like these went through my mind on a beautiful Sunday afternoon as I made my way towards a ship tied up at the river-side of the King George V Dock in Glasgow. I was hoping to persuade a few seamen to come to the Gospel Meeting at our church later that day. Perhaps, I was thinking, most of the crew would be at the Braehead Shopping Centre nearby, it being a Sunday afternoon.

There was not a soul about as I went up the gangway and made my way down the main passageway of the ship. As I reached a steep stairway leading to a lower deck, I heard the murmur of voices, so I went down the iron stairway and found the voices came from behind a door at the foot of the stairs. I gently opened the door and saw about 10 men sitting round a table. I told them who I was and they quickly told me their story. They were a Polish crew and, yesterday (Saturday afternoon) the thirty eight-year-old Captain of their ship, had decided to go into Glasgow City Centre. It was now Sunday and he had not yet returned to the ship. They were worried. I tried to play it down by telling them that there were a lot of Polish people in the Glasgow area because of the many Polish troops who had been in Scotland during WWII and had married Scottish girls and stayed on in Scotland. Perhaps, I said, the Captain was away visiting Polish relatives or friends. They were not convinced, and I felt that they were holding back their own thoughts on the matter. They did not want to say too much or confess their worst fears. None of them wanted to come to the Gospel Meeting that evening so I left them some literature. The next day (Monday) I went back to the ship. When I arrived at the docks, there was police activity around the ship and the police divers were searching the river. I spoke to one of the police officers on the quayside about the possibility of the Captain having Polish relatives in Scotland – but the police officer pointed to the river and said bluntly, "He will be in there."

The next day the Captain's wife arrived from Poland – but there was still no solution to the mystery of his disappearance. Towards the end of the week, however, the police divers departed. The Captain's body had been found in the murky river. I never heard the full story of his death. My own theory was that the Captain had gone into the city centre, returning to the ship late in the evening. The gangway, as is often the case at night, would be drawn up for reasons of security. He would have tried to get aboard but, missed his footing and fallen into the water. Or perhaps he had got aboard all right but had taken ill and fallen overboard.

The Bible tells us, in Psalm 107, of a great storm where the seamen were at their wits' end in a ship that was sinking, but they cried to God and He saved them out of all their trouble.

How will you fair in the storms of the year?
If you're anchored in Jesus, you've nothing to fear.

Absent Without Leave

The large ocean-going tug, was registered in Cornwall. I had passed it a few times but somehow I had never boarded it – it always seemed deserted.

However, when I drove past one day two men were working on deck. I stopped and spoke to them. One of the men, wearing a bushy moustache, was William the Captain. He told me they were up in Glasgow to do a towing job to England but they would have to wait for suitable weather as it was the month of December and rather stormy; it is a dangerous job to tow a ship in stormy weather. I met William again when I visited the docks the following day. He told me the crew of five had been sent home until the weather improved. He would phone them and they could come up to Glasgow by plane in a couple of hours. William was standing by on the ship alone. He told me he wasn't feeling very well, with a pain in his stomach. I said I would keep in touch with him and I gave him my phone number. I visited the ship each day for several days and still he complained of pain.

Then one Sunday he phoned me to say he could not stand the pain any longer and during the night he had phoned the hospital and they had referred him to a local emergency clinic, and would I take him there. By this time he was doubled up and could hardly walk. At the clinic the doctor examined him and told him to go to the local hospital the next day.

I returned to the ship the next day to take him to the Southern General Hospital, which was close to the docks, but he did not seem to be around. I went down below where the cabins were located but it was pitch dark. I tried to switch on the lights but everything had been cut off at the main switch. I groped my way around in the dark shouting "William, William are you there? William, are you all right?"

I stumbled my way into all the cabins and checked the beds in each of them pulling at the bedclothes to see if anyone was lying in bed. I shouted again, "It's Sam!" but there was no response. I began to think he may be lying somewhere seriously ill, or maybe even dead. I went through all the corners systematically but I could find no one. I listened, I shouted, but when I stopped shouting there was dead silence. I began to panic a little at the lack of response. Could he be in the river, I wondered? I went back up on deck and stood around for a short time wondering what to do, but, finally, went home. Where was he? Should I go to the police? I went over the possibilities in my mind. Maybe he had got up early and got a taxi and gone to the hospital on his own. I enquired at the hospital but they could not trace anyone of his name. I decided to wait.

Christmas came and went – and then one day I decided to take another look and drove down to the docks. I saw the ship was still berthed in its usual place – and, drawing near, saw William standing on the deck as right as rain! Trying to sound calm, I shouted from the quayside: "What happened?" "I decided to go home," he said, "so I took a taxi to the airport and got a plane home." He seemed unaware of how worried I had been. He had not thought to inform me of what he was going to do – although it was possible he had lost my phone number. My words "Am I glad to see you!" came from the heart! And with that, I moved on to the next ship!

Anchored In Jesus

The twinkling lights of the ship I was making for came from Berth No. 10 – at the far end of the docks and about a mile and a half from the security gate. It was a Sunday evening in the middle of December, a dark frosty night, with a gale blowing. What a night to be out in my old Honda car! It was difficult to steer in the driving rain that blew up from the dark, forbidding river.

I was on a mission to collect three Dutch seamen from the gangway of their ship. They had promised to come to church. It was pitch dark, with no moon or star to be seen.

The docks in Glasgow are very isolated and on a night like this it was a bleak and eerie "no man's land". Not much chance of seeing a human being or hearing a sound – just the fierce roaring of the wind. It reminded me of Psalm 107 in the Bible where it tells of a terrible storm. As I drove through dockland at about five miles an hour watching out for the many potholes and the old railway lines I suddenly saw a movement in the headlights. Something was crossing in front of me. I speeded up a bit and saw a large fox scampering into one of the sheds. If the car got water-logged or had a puncture, I would be in real trouble. What a night! Sometimes on occasions like this the thought crossed my mind that I must be crazy to come here on a night like this in the dead of winter – and alone. But I was glad I was never afraid. I had been coming to the docks for around 15 years and I give thanks to the Lord that I have kept faith in my God. I have trusted Him all the way and, in spite of some difficulties, I have never thought of quitting. I remembered that God had said to

Gideon, Moses and Joshua, when He assigned them really big and fearful jobs – "Go, and I will be with you." And He never forsook them. It is the Lord's work and when He gives you a task He equips you to do that task. I can truly say he has proved that with me in the deep darkness and loneliness of these docks and in boarding a thousand ships. He has given me courage that I never thought I had – and health and strength to do what He has allotted me to do. I give Him all the glory.

I approached the Dutch ship, sheltering in my car from the wind and rain. I stopped the car and waited for the Dutch seamen who had promised to meet me. They did not appear; I waited for some time and still they did not appear. I pumped the horn - but finally drove off, thinking that the seamen had decided to remain in their warm mess room on such a stormy night.

All Wrapped Up!

One day I received a phone call from my friend, Tom, a director of a large bus company. He told me the company name had changed and, as a result, they had been left with a lot of uniforms which had the old logo embroidered on them. Could I take them and make use of them amongst the seamen? I told him I would be very happy to have the clothing. He told me everything was new and in good condition. The bus depot was about twenty miles from Glasgow and he said he would arrange for the store to be open on whatever day I could come.

My friend, Bert, and I hired a van and, along with Bert's grandson, Jamie, who was spending his holidays with his grandparents, we made our way to the bus depot. We were delighted with what we saw. All the clothes were navy blue – an ideal colour. The pullovers and jackets and trousers were of good quality. There were ties and gloves and socks. Everything was suitable for the seamen – except perhaps the Inspectors' peaked caps! We loaded up the van and brought all the clothes to my house where I sorted everything out into the various sizes. For the next couple of years, I carefully shared the clothing amongst seamen of many nationalities. Sometimes I had problems in fitting the seamen with their correct sizes and had to give them as near their right size as possible.

But seamen are not fussy when it comes to clothing, especially in winter. It is so cold at sea at that time of year they are grateful for good warm clothes – even if the fit is not perfect! For many of the seamen I was able to give them a full kit of trousers and jacket and pullover and socks and even a tie – all with the old bus company logo!

I remember kitting out an elderly Filipino, called Angelo. He was the assistant cook. He was delighted with what he got and went to his cabin to change. Everything fitted well and he came back on deck to show them off. I had brought with me one of the Inspectors' peaked caps which no one had shown much interest in. I said to him "You are assistant cook?" "Yes!" he said. I then took out the Inspector's cap and placed it on his head, "You are now Captain Cook!" I said. This caused great hilarity all round, Angelo's laughter being the loudest.

When the laughter had subsided, I reminded the crew to look at the Christian literature and Bibles I had left on the mess room table. Soon they were all gathered round the table sharing what was on offer.

The Amber

This large ship had twenty of a crew, all Burmese, with a Greek Captain. I was a little bit apprehensive in boarding this large Greek ship. I remembered that the Burmese are mostly Buddhist.

However, I climbed aboard and, when I finally found the mess room, they all seemed very interested, and welcomed me. When I spread out my literature on a table, they crowded round. They surprised me because most of them were quite good readers and speakers of English. They looked a rough lot, but they were very friendly.

They gave me coffee and biscuits and, when I gave them woolly hats, they then offered to give me dinner! I gave them some good clothing too. They took lots of literature, including some Burmese language tracts I had in my bag. They were very open to the gospel.

Next day I returned with more Burmese language leaflets and clothing. A lot of them asked for Bibles and asked me to write my name on the Bibles and the name of the port, and the date. All had good manners and worked hard at their various jobs. Some of them were covered in grease from the engine room. They gave me little presents of pictures and ornaments and a large pennant of Burma. We had a great chat about Burma when the British Army fought against the Japanese and about the battles of Kohima and Imphal, near the Indian border – which was the turning-point in the battle for Burma and the retaking of the country from the Japanese. The British Army had been helped all the way by Burmese fighters, loyal to the British. I asked about Christianity in Burma and some of them were able to tell me of Christian missionaries which I was able to substantiate when I made enquiries at a later date when I became friendly with a young Burmese Christian on a Korean ship. Sadly, this young Burmese Christian man later died in a tragic accident while his ship was in Japan.

They also talked of Adoniram Judson, an early Christian missionary in Burma. He was from America. All-in-all, it was a great visit and I hoped to meet some more Burmese crew at a later date.

I was quite sorry for these young men. I took three of them to the Sunday evening gospel service and I invited them to my home for supper. They were very thankful for my visit and could hardly believe that everything was free.

I left the ship with feelings of a worthwhile visit.

M/V Panda

There was a Dutch ship in dock. As I went up the gangway I noticed two men painting something on the funnel of the ship. When I told them who I was, one them said he was a Christian but he was finding it very hard and difficult as he was the only Christian on the ship and said if only he had one Christian friend he would be happy. I encouraged him and told him Jesus was the best and most faithful friend he could ever have. I gave him a calendar and a Seed Sower's text to put up in his cabin and said it would remind him of the Lord Jesus who suffered and died for him on the Cross.

He said the ship was his home, and as I left, they continued with their painting. I noticed it was a sketch of an animal. I asked them what kind of animal it was. He said it was a panda, because that was the name of the ship. I saw it finished when I went back the next day. They certainly had made a very good job of it. The panda looked very beautiful – as all pandas are in their black and white coats.

The Americans Are Back

A strange thing happened at the docks in the year 2009: an American ship came in. Nothing too unusual about that – except that it had been eight years since an American ship had come in to Glasgow. Before that, American ships came in to Glasgow regularly. But all that ended after a US ship was attacked in Yemen and several US sailors killed by terrorists. And, then, the terrorist attack in 2001 on the Twin Towers in New York finally ensured that no US ships would return. They had become nervous and thought Glasgow Dock was not secure enough for US ships – so that was it. They moved to Portsmouth in the south of England – a port they felt was more secure.

I was sorry, because I had got on very well with the Americans in years gone by. A number of them had come to the Gospel Meeting at our church. I always picked them up at their ship by car at six o'clock on the Sunday evening. In the days before they left for Portsmouth a boom was erected across the dock basin to prevent any small boats coming in during the hours of darkness – and the crew were on constant patrol with guns at the ready.

Anyone near the American ship was treated with suspicion. It reminded me of my old army days in the Far East. A shout would greet me even though they knew who I was: "Halt! Who goes there?" "Friend!" I would answer. "Advance and be recognised!" would be the reply and a revolver pointed at me. They would look at the name on my hard hat and would say "Pass friend!" I imagined Americans in situations like this being rather trigger-happy. They made me as nervous as they seemed to be themselves!

Now, after eight years, they had returned – but the scene had changed again. The security man at the gate of the docks told me that there were 4 ships docked and one of them was an American ship – but, he added, "You probably won't get near it, never mind board it." I decided to try. As I approached, I saw that the ship was guarded and surrounded by a high wire fence on the quayside to keep visitors out. In front of that was a security cabin and the man on guard told me he was from a local security firm. It was raining heavily and he invited me into his hut and we chatted for a while. I decided to test his reaction and said that I would like to approach the ship and see if I could board it. He did not seem to object. I was about to hoist my bag on to my back when he said "You would be better to leave your bag here – they might think it contains a bomb." He pressed his point: "I don't think you would get on while carrying that bag." I thought this was good advice, but there was not much point in going aboard without my bag. I was not going simply to inspect the ship but to give them good Christian literature that could enrich their lives and lead them to God.

As I moved off, the security man said, "You will likely be back in about 15 minutes". In a few minutes I reached the gangway – so far so good. The two guards from the top of the gangway were sizing me up. I hoped that I did not look too much of a threat. Americans are permitted to carry a gun and, if they think there is a threat, they are permitted to use it and ask questions afterwards. The two men were not in uniform. I climbed slowly up the gangway with this bulky-looking bag over my shoulder. I got to the top without a warning shot being fired. I shook hands with both of them and then announced myself, pointing to the words on my hard hat which read "Port Mission".

I quickly opened my bag and let them see what it contained: Bibles, calendars, Emmaus Courses, large Seed Sowers' texts, tracts, etc. They seemed quite interested and willing to chat. They told me the crew were mostly American naval personnel. Another man came on the scene. He said he was a Christian and that he would be happy to come to the Gospel Service on the forthcoming Sunday – until one of the guards pointed to a notice pinned up on a nearby board saying that the ship was leaving on Sunday.

Shortly after this, the Ship's Doctor appeared on the scene. He was very interested in Christian things and invited me to join him for dinner that evening. But I told him I was already soaked with the heavy rain and, having no car (I was not allowed to drive following a stroke), I had a long way to go home. The Ship's Doctor accompanied me back to the security cabin where the security man seemed relieved to see me. The Doctor tried again to get me to stay for dinner but I could feel the rain running down my back. So I bade him goodbye and a safe journey and began my long tramp round the deserted dock in the last light of the day to wait for the bus to appear. But it was all worth while – the Americans were back.

The Ancient Mariners

This was one of the few ships I came across with an all-British crew. It was not a very big ship, having only about six or seven of a crew. It came in regularly to Glasgow and I visited it often and got on well with the crew. I thought they all seemed to be quite elderly to be active seamen.

They always made me welcome. The Captain liked to chat to me, mostly about Ireland. He himself was a genial Irishman from Co. Down. The cook was a tall thin man with glasses, from London, and every lunch time he cooked the same thing: bacon and eggs, sausages, black pudding, and fried dumpling, with plenty of Heinz beans! I told him about fried potato scones, which we sometimes have in Scotland, and he promised to add these to his menu as soon as he could get some. He always offered me the lunch too but I was wary of this dish, popularly known in Glasgow as "a heart attack on a plate". I took coffee only and, sometimes, soup. He said the Captain liked his soup with a couple of Oxo Cubes in it!

They always dressed like "down and outs". They never shaved, and they all had long beards and long hair, and some had pony tails, and one or two went about with bare feet and shorts. I gave them plenty of clothing and shoes but most never seemed to wear them. I gave the Captain a heavy Aran knit roll neck jersey. It was white, and he loved it. It gave him a distinctive look apart from the crew.

I tried to get some of them to come to the gospel service on a Sunday evening. They never said "No" but none of them ever came. I told them about God and Jesus. They were happy to take Christian calendars and large John 3:16 texts, and I usually left them various gospel leaflets. One or two of the crew never said a word to me at any time; they just looked and listened. They looked like seamen that had run aground on a Pacific island a long number of years previously and had only recently been rescued by a passing ship. The only break-through I had with them spiritually was one day when I noticed the Captain had one of my Christian calendars pinned up in his room. The text on it for the month was: Jesus said, "Come unto Me all you that labour and are heavy laden, and I will give you rest."

I have not seen this ship for a number of years now but I have often wondered about them. May God bless them wherever they may be.

The Barras

This small ship was one of the few British ships I have encountered during my 15 years at Glasgow Docks. It was a nice little ship that came into Glasgow occasionally. The Captain was a very pleasant man from Cornwall. When we met, he talked of moral problems and their solutions and how the attitude to Christian values had changed so much.

He took some literature but did not want a Bible; he said he already had a Bible – but as I was leaving the ship, he suddenly asked for a Bible. He said, "For my wife!" I was happy to give him a New Testament – which was easier to read than the entire Bible – but I wondered if it was really for himself that he was asking (although he had told me that he already had a Bible).

Such an attitude is quite common, not only in seamen. I encountered it when knocking on doors to distribute Christian literature in Govan, Glasgow. If it was a man who answered my knock he would say, "O.K. – I will take your Bible and give it to my wife." It is a sort of "macho" thing.

The attitude is: a man like me does not need a Bible. I am not a cissie, I'm a sailor! I'm tough! I thought to myself: I'm a Glasgow man - and I'm certainly not tough!

This attitude is not always restricted to men. I remember one time my wife and I went to "The Barras" one Saturday afternoon. The Barras, and the nearby Paddy's Market, are situated in the East End of Glasgow. The Barras consists of a large area of wasteland containing hundreds of barrows and market stalls, selling second-hand clothing and everything under the sun. Paddy's Market is situated in a lane near The Barras but has no stalls or barrows, the goods for sale lying on the ground. In fact I believe at the time of writing, Paddy's Market has gone due to re-development. In the past as well as the market traders, many outdoor showmen frequented both these places. One example was a man who sold "mystery parcels" containing, he said, a cigarette lighter and a coat hanger for 3p – and when the parcel was opened up by the buyer, it was found to contain a two inch nail (the coat hanger) and a humble match (the cigarette lighter)!

Many people spent a whole day at The Barras and it provided a great day out at no cost (unless some purchases were made from the stalls).

After my wife and I visited The Barras we felt in need of a nice cup of tea. A short walk from The Barras was a church with a board outside advertising teas and home baking. We decided to have a cup of tea and a piece of home baked cake. The money was collected at the till by an elderly lady sitting at a table. As we were paying, I said to her in general conversation, "You're doing a good job!" "Aye," she said, "I've been doing this for eleven years." "Well," I said, jokingly "you'll get your reward in heaven!"

The Bottle Thrower

I visited King George V Dock one cold winter afternoon. The whole place was deserted – except for a ship that had not long berthed. The security chain was across the gangway but I hung about for a while hoping that someone would appear. A cold wind blew in from the river as I waited for something to happen - and I was not disappointed.

A big rough-looking man suddenly appeared on the deck of the ship holding a bottle and waved his arms around. I shouted up to him, and lifted my bag in a series of up-and-down motions. He shouted "No, no, no want" and threw the bottle towards me. It smashed near my feet. I moved forward and kicked the broken glass into the river. He may not have been trying to hit me with the bottle, but I was not going to give him another chance to target me, so I moved towards my car to go home. But I changed my mind, stopped, and opened my bag and took out a handful of literature – calendars, large Seed Sowers' texts, etc. - and waved it in his direction. He did not seem too interested, so I took out a handful of hats given to me by a ladies knitting group. "For you!" I shouted. "Free. No money!" I put one on my head and he laughed.

He came over to the gangway and unclipped the security chain and signalled me to board the ship. I gave him a hat and a calendar and asked him where he was from. "Poland!" he said. I then gave him a Polish language New Testament. He never said a word. I pressed home my advantage: "Mess room!" I said. He pointed to a door and down a stair. I eventually found the mess room and explained who I was to a group of about eight men.

They made me welcome and gave me soup and coffee. I was glad of the soup to heat me up as I was feeling very cold. I put all my literature on the table and encouraged everyone to help themselves. "You take some," I said. "All free. No money."

I have met a few evangelical Polish Christians but most Poles are devout Catholics. One Polish man from another ship asked me for a Thomson's Chain Reference Bible. I found one in a well-known evangelical bookshop but they wanted about £60 for it, which was too much for me. I tried other second hand bookshops and eventually got one – but by this time the ship had gone, and another Christian seaman, from another ship, got the benefit of it.

The Polish ship never came in again, that I know of. As for the bottle-thrower, I never saw him again but he got some literature and a hat.

Pray for these poor sailors, sailing the wide oceans of the world with all its dangers – lonely and far from home.

The Boxers

I met Marina on board a Russian ship. She was a friendly girl of about twenty. There was quite a number of the crew in the mess room when I introduced myself and laid out the Christian literature on a table, as I did on every ship. Marina was among the crew. I gave a general invitation to come to church the following Sunday. Marina could speak some English and she indicated she would like to come. I said I would come for her at 18.00 hours. She said she would have to get permission from the Captain as he did not like to see her going out alone in a strange country. After about 15 minutes she returned, accompanied by the Captain. I think he wanted to check up on me! He must have been reassured because he said it would be all right for her to go - and he asked the Second Officer if he would go also. When I called at the ship on the Sunday Marina and the Second Officer were waiting for me. The whole church welcomed her and she got on well with everyone.

She and the Second Officer joined my wife and me at our home for supper after church and they seemed to enjoy themselves. We sang some hymns too, which they liked.

Next day I went back to the ship and the Captain was happy that the two members of his crew had been well-received - and he gave me dinner!

Afterwards, two of the crew approached me with a rather unusual request – could I find for them a full-sized boxing ring, so that they could do some training? I could easily see that they were boxers – one may have had a broken nose and the other appeared to have a cauliflower ear! On my way home, I called in at Bellahouston Sports Centre and enquired about boxing facilities. I was surprised when the attendant showed me a room with a full-sized boxing ring and all the necessary equipment – gloves, punch bags, etc. He said it would cost only a small fee seeing it was for seamen from a ship on a visit to Glasgow, and only for a week. I took the seamen there on the first day and after that they went on their own every day for a week. They sailed away happy men, one sporting a new black eye!

On this ship, also, the Navigating Officer told me he was a historian and was interested in the history of Scotland. He knew about "Mr. Wallace" and would like to see "his castle and monument in Stirling". He asked me how to get there and how far away it was. I told him it was about 37 miles from Glasgow and he could get a bus from Buchanan Bus Station in Glasgow City Centre. It was a good service and it would take one hour. I saw him about a couple of days later and he told me he had had a great time in Stirling. Then he asked how he could get to see the Loch Ness Monster! I told him Loch Ness was about 132 miles away, near the town of Inverness, and it would be too far for him to travel there as his ship was sailing in a couple of days. I told him instead to visit Glasgow's museums. They were all free. He agreed to do this and was happy to find out much about the history of Scotland in the museums. He sailed away with a bagful of leaflets and brochures. I presented him with a Bible in his own Russian language and I told him that, as he was interested in history, he could read in the Bible the history of Jesus Christ and about His wonderful plan of salvation.

The Brave Aberdonian

The small German ship had a tall German Captain and a crew of three Polish seamen and four Filipinos. The Captain was a very pleasant young man. We had a long talk about many things. I offered him Christian literature and told him to help himself from what I had laid out on the table of the mess room as everything was free.

The Filipinos took extra John 3:16 Seed Sowers' texts. These are very popular and attractive and I sometimes put them into 10 x 8 frames which I get from a local shopping centre in Glasgow for £1 each. They make a very attractive and colourful picture of this lovely verse. I tell the seamen that it is the best-known verse in the Bible. The only thing I don't like about putting the texts in frames is that the reverse side of the text is then hidden. The reverse side gives the reader a gospel message explaining the meaning of the text. However, I get round this by telling them to take some of the unframed texts along with the framed one. I get the Seed Sowers' texts from Canada where they are published by a group of Christians.

I usually order a full box which contains 1100. They are sent free of charge. I had been getting them from an agent in Scotland, a Christian man called Malcolm Radcliffe. He has now moved to Northern Ireland. I now get them from a Christian man in England who is the new agent for the UK.

I also receive from Canada a CD of hymns relating to the sea – which are very appropriate to my mission among seamen. An accompanying "musical" background is supplied by the sound of the waves and the calling of the seagulls. Well-known gospel hymns are sung by a young Irishman whose family are missionaries in Canada. He sings that good old nautical hymn, *Over the Deadline Tonight,* and others, such as *Will Your Anchor Hold, The Haven of Rest, Shelter in the Storm, When Peace Like a River, Amazing Grace,* and *Let the Lower Lights Be Burning.*

A short gospel message is included in the CD. It tells the story of a ship with a crew of 14 Lithuanians that left Glasgow on a very stormy night and ran into trouble in the stormy waters of the North of Scotland. The ship was called "The Green Lily". Battered by huge waves, in a force 10 gale, "The Green Lily" sent out a mayday signal for help. A Coast Guard helicopter picked up their signal and eventually found the sinking ship. Despite the huge waves, and great danger, it got near enough to lower the winchman, Bill Deacon from Aberdeen, down on to the sloping deck of the ship. Bill first of all secured himself bodily to the rail of the ship because of the great risk of being blown overboard. He then began hooking up the first man of the fourteen-man crew, ready for lifting to the helicopter. Once the first man reached the helicopter, the winch was lowered again and Bill continued to secure each seaman until he reached the last man. As the winch was being lowered for Bill to be taken up to the helicopter, he loosened the rope from the handrail and was waiting for the winch to reach him when a huge wave swept him to his death in the wild and stormy sea. For his bravery, Bill Deacon was posthumously awarded the George Medal.

The CD ends with the gospel story of the Lord Jesus giving his life on the cross at Calvary for all those who put their trust in Him for salvation.

"For God so loved the world
That He gave his only begotten Son
That whosoever believeth in Him
Should not perish
But have everlasting life."
John 3:16

The Burmese Singers

I drove to the docks one fine summer morning and made my way towards a ship that had just arrived that morning. Before I reached the ship, I noticed three young seamen walking towards the gatehouse, obviously intent on having a look at their new Scottish surroundings. I pulled up beside them, told them who I was, and asked them where they came from. "From Burma!" they said, and explained that they were going to the nearby Braehead Shopping Centre. As they were strangers, I told them to jump into my car and I would take them to the shops.

I turned the car round and began driving the short distance to Braehead Shopping Centre. As I drove, I was surprised when the Burmese seamen began to sing one of my favourite hymns:

> I have decided to follow Jesus,
>   No turning back,
>   No turning back.

The tune was catchy and I joined in . . . . . but I only knew the first two verses . . . . . whereas they carried right on and sang four verses! Before it was time to get off at Braehead they had agreed to come to the gospel service on Sunday evening, and had promised to bring with them the four verses of the complete hymn. I asked them how they had come to learn that hymn and they told me that they had learnt it at the YMCA in Belfast when their ship was in Belfast Dock. They had liked it so much they had written the words down before they left that city. They were very happy to meet up with me – two of them were Christians, and the third was a Muslim – and it was great to hear the Muslim lad singing as loudly as the other two!

We often sing hymns with seamen of many nationalities – *Jesus Loves Me This I Know; Will Your Anchor Hold In The Storms Of Life; Give Me Oil In My Lamp* and *In The Sweet By and By.*

After the gospel meeting, the three seamen came back to our house for supper – and more singing (all seamen love to sing when they get the chance!). It was on that same night, also, that our friends, Ian and Moira Stewart, came for supper. They also are good singers – so we all had a great time praising the Lord!

A friend once gave me a present of a nice guitar (in return for some joiner-work I did for her!) and when I bring the seamen to the house I always ask if anyone can play the guitar. Often a seaman will volunteer to play, especially the men from the Pacific Islands of Kiribati and Tuvalu (although the finest player of the guitar was Naomi Keyser, the wife of American preacher Keith Keyser who was invited to dinner at our house!). Many Filipinos are good at playing the guitar, but rather shy when it comes to singing – but the men from the Pacific Isles love to sing and it is a joy to hear their harmonious voices. Although they are big men, they have lovely soft voices. Sometimes the Pacific Islanders give me presents of beautiful necklaces for men and women made out of shells and beads.

I usually pass them on to the ladies who help me in the Lord's work by knitting woolly hats and scarves.

The Cape Verde Man

When I board a ship, I introduce myself, and when I get to the mess room I spread out on a table the literature I have brought with me: Bible courses, large Seed Sowers' texts, tracts, calendars, Bibles – most of the literature available in a number of languages. I urge the seamen to take extra home to their families – mother and father, wife, children, brothers and sisters. Thousands of men from all over the world, from Poland, Russia, the Philippines, Burma, China, Pacific Islands, have been happy to accept Christian literature and copies of the written word of God.

Many have taken Emmaus Bible Courses – a great source of learning about Christian things – plain reading, simple and straight-forward questions to test understanding. The Emmaus Bible School in Liverpool has been very good to me in my dealings with them, giving me a 30% discount on all courses.

My way of giving them to interested seamen is to put each course in a suitably-sized unsealed envelope which I address to myself, but without a stamp, not knowing what country they would post them back to me from. When the completed course is returned to me I correct the answers and award them a percentage out of 100. I then send the result to the Emmaus offices in Liverpool for a laminated certificate and an enamel badge with the letters EBS inscribed on it. I send these back to the participant and congratulate him on his success. Sometimes it is years before I receive the finished course – but often it is much quicker!

One man from the Cape Verde Islands, off the west coast of

Africa, accepted an Emmaus Course. His ship was in Glasgow for one day only and was leaving the following day at ten o'clock in the morning. At eight o'clock on the morning of the ship's departure he arrived at my house in a taxi to deliver the completed Emmaus Bible Course I had given him the day before! He said he had stayed up all night to finish the course and wanted to make sure I received it safely. Some of the courses contain as many as 100 questions and for a poor African man from Cape Verde to complete and deliver the course in one evening was no mean task. In the short time he was at my house he took time to have breakfast, and I gave him some good clothes and a pair of shoes. I made sure he was back at his ship in time for its departure that morning – and I did not forget to send him his Certificate and badge!

Some seamen do not do very well in answering the questions, mostly because of language difficulties. I take this into account when marking their answers and am sympathetic with my score – to encourage them to go on to the next course.

Cape Verde is an island off the coast of Senegal in West Africa. I always got on well with the Cape Verde seamen and found them very kind and pleasant. Unfortunately, with the break up of the Soviet Union, many shipping companies stopped employing Cape Verde men. This is because of the location of the islands: 400 miles off the coast of Africa. When returning home, the seamen had to take a plane to Africa and then a ship for 400 miles to their island home – all paid for by the shipping company. Thus it became too expensive to fly them home at the end of their contract. Now seamen from Poland, Russia, Ukraine and Lithuania have replaced the men from Cape Verde.

Most of the seamen I have met show great respect for the Word of God and the literature I give them.

The Crystal Orb

When I climbed the gangway of this fish factory ship with the strange-sounding name, little did I know that I would be climbing this same gangway, several days a week, for the next six months. It was not a large ship but it contained sixty-two of a crew – all from Romania. The ship was rusty and generally neglected and looked in a bad way.

I told the first man I met that I was the Port Missionary and he said, in broken English, "You must speak to the Captain. I take you there now." The Captain made me welcome and proceeded to give me a tale of woe. The company that owned the ship was bankrupt. No wages had been paid for quite a long time. No one on the ship had any money; everyone was skint. Food was very scarce too. They were presently waiting for money for food from the Romanian authorities – but that might take several days. The Captain was due to hold a meeting with the crew in fifteen minutes to explain the latest position to them - and he invited me to join him at the meeting.

The crew had gathered in the mess room. The Captain told them what he had told me. There was no money available and hardly any food. I thought the crew took the news quite calmly – perhaps they had half-expected it. The Captain then introduced me to them as the Glasgow Port Missionary. I told them I would help them all I could and hoped to bring some food the next day. I told them a bit about Glasgow. They could walk to the city centre in about 45 minutes. There were plenty of good museums – all with free entry - and plenty of libraries – and the church I went to was only one kilometre from the docks. They would not have to worry about money there as they did not take any collection! We were open every Sunday and Wednesday – and they would be welcome. I also told them I would be able to supply them with good second-hand clothing and good Christian literature, Bibles and Bible Courses. I lifted their spirits and they gave me a rousing cheer.

When I got home, I phoned up some of my friends with the news. They soon began to supply me with jars of coffee, tea and bread, milk and eggs and chicken and cheese. I went to the ship the next day with the boot of my Ford Sierra well-filled with food supplies. The Captain and the officers were delighted. They told me the Seamen's Union had given them some money to buy food until they got a regular income. I told them they would be o.k. as I knew of a giant bulk-buying food superstore where the seamen would get a good deal for their money. This superstore proved a great help to the Crystal Orb seamen. When money became available, my Ford Sierra car worked overtime visiting the superstore. Two of the ship's officers and the cook would set off with me and load the car to capacity to feed the sixty hungry seamen. An example of the shopping would be about 200 chickens, 500 eggs, huge blocks of Cheddar cheese, large cans of cooking oil, dozens of 1 cwt bags of potatoes, and onions. Each visit, the bill amounted to hundreds of pounds. Their check-out slips were about 5 metres long! Sometimes we had to make several journeys in the one week. Even a famous fish and chip shop in Glasgow got to know of their plight and decided to gain some publicity by delivering free fish suppers to the ship's company.

It was a summer of warm sunshine and many of the seamen got to know Glasgow very well and would go to charity shops and jumble sales to buy clothes at reasonable prices. They made these into huge parcels sewn up in canvass to send to their relatives in Romania. I would squeeze these 40 kilo parcels into my car and take them to the local Post Office for dispatch to Romania.

Sometimes the parcels were over the stipulated weight, so rather than take them back to the ship we would unpack them in the Post Office to make them lighter – and people coming in to buy stamps, etc. would smile and say "I didn't know there was a jumble sale in the Post Office today!" However, the seamen had no complaint and continued to send the parcels home.

Some of the seamen walked into the town every day. Others became regular attenders at our church every Wednesday and Sunday.

Soon we had our annual church outing to Pitlochry and I arranged for a few of the seamen to join us and also to attend the Sunday School trip the following week to David Livingstone's birthplace at Blantyre.

As time passed, it seemed as if the crew of the Crystal Orb would be with us for ever – but then one day, quite suddenly, they were issued with one-way airline tickets from Glasgow to Bucharest. They were leaving from Glasgow Airport the next Friday morning!

A farewell supper in the mess room was arranged for the night before they left and I was invited to attend. My wife, Wilma, was a little anxious about this. She thought that it might turn into a drunken rabble - but I had come to know these men well and I assured her that all would be well. These men had endured being stuck for months in a rusty old ship in bad and unhealthy conditions. Most had maintained a respectful and cheerful attitude. There had been very few problems of drunkenness or disorderly behaviour. They had been away from home in a foreign port where they could easily have run into trouble – but there had been no trouble.

On the night of the farewell party the Captain invited me to dinner with the ship's officers. We then moved down to the mess room where the crew were already assembled. As a token of appreciation for what I had done for them, I was presented with a beautiful wrist watch, and several smaller gifts. One was a set of new windscreen wipers for my car (someone had noticed that my existing wipers were not performing very well and needed replacing!). I thanked them for everything and spoke to them a word in the gospel about going home. I told him that the Christian believer's home is in heaven. I read to them John 14 "Let not your heart be troubled," said Jesus "in my Father's house are many mansions. I go to prepare a place for you." I told them it had been a great pleasure to know them and asked them not to forget what they had learned while they had been in Glasgow. I gave some of the crew the address of a missionary I knew who was resident in Brazov, Romania. Later, when they returned home, several of the crew wrote me letters of thanks and appreciation. I still keep in touch with some of the seamen.

The Crystal Orb and the Creepy Crawlies

The ship was now infested with vermin. Whenever I visited the ship they would give me coffee and biscuits but the cockroaches and bugs and all kinds of moving insects were intent on devouring every loose crumb as it fell. We had to eat with one hand, and keep a rolled-up newspaper in the other to slay the bugs and insects that crawled all over the place!

I noticed one day that Morrow had a large plaster on the back of his neck. He never said why it was there, so, one day, I asked him if I could have a look. He agreed, and I managed to tear the plaster to one side, along with some uprooted hair, and was confronted with a mass of huge suppurating boils. I put the plaster back and said he had better to come with me to the hospital.

We waited a long time at the Accident & Emergency Department of the local hospital (it was a busy Friday night). When our turn came, we were called into a small room. Shortly, a doctor came in and tore off the plaster - and then stuck it back on again, and went out without saying a word. This was repeated some time later by another doctor. Finally, a woman doctor came in, took one look at Morrow's neck, tut-tut-ed, and said "This will have to be scrubbed and drained! We will have to keep you in hospital to treat this!" She also murmured something about blood-poisoning. By this time, it was nearly mid-night. When I arrived home, my wife was in a panic as we were due to go on holiday the next day – and I had failed to phone her to say what was happening! Poor Morrow was kept in hospital for five days, and then had to attend a local clinic in Govan. They treated him there for some weeks – but one day the doctor called me over to tell me he would have to send Morrow home to Romania as the boils were spreading down his back and healing would take a long time.

So Morrow was dispatched on a plane back to Romania shortly thereafter - but I later heard he recovered well - so the story had a happy ending!

The Crystal Orb
– Irritation on Board Ship

Only old Peteric and Daniel were left. Peteric tried his best to do the cooking. One day he complained about a rash and a terrible itch in his arms and legs. I mentioned this to a friend of mine who said he would come to the ship to see if he could help Peteric. The first thing he did when he entered the cabin was to lift a half-full jar of coffee that was lying on Peteric's table and throw it out of the porthole into the river – at the same time shouting "No coffee! No coffee! No more coffee!" And to emphasise this further he shouted "Not a drop!" He examined Peteric's arms and legs and then brought out packets of pills and bottles of lotion and proceeded to give Peteric complicated instructions about what to do with them. Some pills were to be taken after meals, some before meals, and at other times the lotion was to be applied. He did not take into account that Peteric was a poor speaker of English. Even I, a native speaker of English, found the instructions hard to follow! Looking round the cabin, he finally left with the words "Remember – no coffee; not a drop!"

Peteric told me afterwards that he had planned to give him a cup of coffee before he left but he was afraid to do so in case he threw his last jar of coffee out of the porthole!

Peteric was missing his old friend Morrow, who had recently returned to Romania, so he decided to return home too. I believe all the pills and potions were given to the giant cockroaches and bugs who carried them away for a farewell dinner (actually they were thrown overboard)!

All the time he was in Glasgow, Peteric attended our church. He just loved to hear the good news of the gospel. In one of his letters to me after he had returned home he told me that he had got baptised in a church in Romania.

I gave some of the seamen the address of Paul Williams the missionary who serves the Lord in Brazov in the north of the country. But I did not hear of any contact. Brazov is a long way from Constanta, the large Baltic Port in the south of the country where most of the seamen come from.

The Crystal Orb
– The Last Farewell

One day Daniel told me that the ship had been sold - and soon after that it was towed away to the scrapyard. I waved it out of the dock in a gesture of farewell. It was like saying goodbye to an old friend. The Crystal Orb had provided a God-given opportunity for showing Christian love in action and spreading the Word of God in the provision of Christian literature.

Daniel went back home to Romania to his wife and children. He was upset about leaving. He had grown to like old Glasgow and had enjoyed his time there. He still keeps in touch with me. Daniel was a very nice man.

The Ship from South Korea

When I arrived at the docks I discovered a Korean ship had arrived since my last visit a few days previously. It was not the first Korean ship that had come into Glasgow but Korean ships were rare. I could see it was a tidy, fair sized, ship. I climbed aboard. The seaman who met me at the top of the gangway was from Burma. I was happy at this because the Burmese seamen that I had previously met had always impressed me. They were good speakers of English and very respectful.

The man on watch at the gangway told me the ship had a Burmese crew but that the officers were all from South Korea. He phoned the Third Officer to announce my arrival. This man soon appeared, dressed in officers' uniform of brown and grey, complete with cap and tie, and he looked very smart. I told him who I was and asked to be shown to the crew's mess room. He invited me to follow him and showed me into a very palatial room with about seven officers all in uniform. Obviously this was the officers' mess. He introduced me and I was given coffee and biscuits. I spread my Christian literature on a large table and enquired if there were any Christians on board. One officer said there was a young Burmese cadet who he thought was a Christian. "I will send for him and you can speak to him."

While we waited, the officers showed great interest in the literature. I told them everything was free and to help themselves. When the young cadet arrived in the room, I observed that he was probably in his late teens, and very smart and efficient-looking. I shook hands with him. He said his name was Yar Zar Nay Win from Rangoon and confirmed he was a Christian. He told me that a Scottish missionary often came out to Burma to visit his church in Rangoon. I asked him the missionary's name but all he could remember was that his name was Andy.

Before I left the officers' mess, I gave them all an invitation to church the following Sunday at 6.30 p.m. Two or three said they would come, and they assured me it would be all right for the cadet, Yar Zar Nay Win, to come with me to church. Before I left the ship, I called in at the Burmese crew's mess room. They were pleased to meet me - and gave me more coffee and biscuits!

On Sunday, I called again at the ship and collected Yar Zar Nay Win but the other officers declined to come. He enjoyed the gospel service and came to our house for supper. He also came to the service on Wednesday evening and, again, to our house. Yar Zar Nay Win was a lovely Christian lad. He told me how his grandfather first became a Christian through the preaching of the gospel by Mr. Judson, an American missionary. His father, a Buddhist, had died two years previously.

Yar Zar Nay Win's mother was a Christian and his young sister of 12 years old, called Nan Dar Nay Win, was getting baptised the following month. My wife, Wilma, sent her a card to celebrate her baptism, and she received a letter in return from the girl – written in Burmese!

One year later, I received a phone call from a man who began by saying that I probably would not know him, but that he knew all about me! I was intrigued by this but my caller soon put me in the picture. His name was Andy McIlree and he lived in Kilmacolm, a village on the outskirts of Glasgow. He is a missionary who has visited Burma on a regular basis for a long number of years. Over many years, he has visited Rangoon and recently he was contacted by a lady who enquired if he knew a Scottish man from Glasgow called Sam Laughlin. Then she showed him a card with my name and address on it which she had found among the papers of her son, Cadet Officer Yar Zar Nay Win.

I was able to tell Andy McIlree that I indeed remembered her son, a very fine Christian Burmese man with whom I had had fellowship while his ship was in Glasgow. Andy had told the young man's mother that he would contact me when he got back to Scotland. It was bad news, Andy McIlree told me. The young seaman had died in a tragic accident while his ship was in Japan.

Andy visited me here in Glasgow and told me what he knew of the accident. Evidently Yar Zar Nay Win had fallen down the iron stair of his ship to his fatal injury.

His mother wrote to me after her son's death and sent me a beautiful picture of her son in his cadet uniform. I was distressed on hearing of his sudden death but I am sure I will meet him in the glory. Yar Zar Nay Win's photograph is on view in my home to this day.

On board ship - on my way to the Messroom.

The Clyde from Jamaica Bridge, Glasgow.

A Mount Everest of a Gangway.

Ship from the Pacific Islands.

A well-known name.

No woolly hats.

Happy with new woolly hats.

Absorbed in a christian calendar.

Romanian group hold meeting.

Dangerous work.

Bible study with Bert Gamble.

Roasting the Christmas Pig.

A helping hand - the literature bag.

Russian ships - three in a row.

Ship visitors to Church in Bethesda Gospel Hall.

Stocking up with food.

Giving God's Word to a mixture of Nations.

Officer Anatoli from Russia.

Some of the Ancient Mariners.

Christian man from Turkey in his Cabin.

Music after supper with new hats.

A Tug leads the way.

The Ship's Barber

When I returned to this ship, which I had been on the previous day, I signalled to the man at the top of the gangway, by lifting my bag up and down, to come down and help me to carry up my bag. He got the message and down he came. When we got to the top of the gangway, and I was signing my name in the Visitors' Book, he asked me (in broken English) "You live in UK?" I said, "Yes, Glasgow!" He said, "Glasgow very far away? I said "No, only six kilometres." I said, "You live far away? Where you live?" He said, "Muscat!" And I said, "In Oman?" He looked at me quite surprised - but he did not know that as a boy I had learned every capital city in the world off by heart. A sailor once asked me if I knew Timbuktu. "Oh, yes," I said. "It's in Africa!"

Going down a passageway on this ship I came across a man giving a haircut and shave to other members of the crew. There was a small queue standing waiting. I took the chance to hand out Christian literature to them while they were waiting. When the barber saw me he said "Ah, Mr. Sam, you would like hair barbered?" "Oh no," I joked, "if you cut my hair you might cut my throat as well!" "Oh no, Mr. Sam, you good man. Your throat not for cutting!" I said, "You good man too. You never cut throats!"

While the queue was waiting, I told them about the preacher who preached a long and very boring sermon. Half-way through the sermon, a young man rose from his seat and began walking out. The preacher halted in mid-sentence and shouted: "Where are you going, boy?" The young man replied, "I'm going for a haircut!" "What?" said the preacher, "could you not have got a haircut before you came in?" "No!" said the young man, "I didn't need a haircut then!"

I don't know if the seamen appreciated the Glasgow-style humour but, nevertheless, they laughed loud and long as this story. I told them that when they had finished getting their hair cut to come to the mess room where I would have lots of Christian literature and woolly hats for them to take home.

The Mercy Ship

The Mercy Ship, named the Anastasia, was a large white British ship. It reminded me of the military hospital ships used during WWII. As I watched the Anastasia on the quayside in Glasgow docks, I recalled the occasion I saw a similar ship one dark night while I was sailing in a troop ship through the Mediterranean in 1944. It was a quiet, balmy evening. I was up on the open deck, leaning on the rail, getting a breath of air away from the hammocks on the lower decks, when I observed in the distance a large ship painted white, with lights blazing, and large red crosses on its sides. It was a British hospital ship, exposed as such to protect it from enemy submarine attacks. They were brave men indeed who sailed in these ships because the German U-boats sometimes did not respect their status and attacked these sitting ducks. I only came across this one on my travels and my heart went out to the sailors who manned the ship and the helpless wounded soldiers aboard. We on the troop ship had at least the protection of our own destroyers that buzzed around our convoy as we sailed along. Also, our ship was camouflaged with no visible lights showing at night-time.

But now the Anastasia was in Glasgow docks and open to the public for two weeks. It sailed mostly to third world countries. There were doctors and dentists and nurses aboard – all volunteers. The ship had operating theatres and treated all kinds of illnesses and diseases.

As I was going round the dock in my car, I saw a man walking towards me. I stopped my car and asked him if he was from the Mercy Ship. He said he was – but only for four or five days.

He had flown from America to visit his daughter who was a volunteer nurse on board ship. He was a very pleasant man and introduced himself as Steve. Sunday being the next day, I asked him if he would like to come to our church to hear the gospel being preached. He was delighted with the invitation so I arranged to pick him up at the ship the next day.

I had also invited some seamen from the Philippines to church, and a Malaysian medical student – so after church, accompanied by our church friends George and Margaret Courtney – we returned to our house with Steve, the three Filipino seamen and our friendly medical student, and enjoyed supper together.

We had a grand old time round the keyboard praising the Lord. During the evening, Steve prayed warmly and with insight. The following Wednesday, he came to our midweek meeting, when the speaker was Charles Geddes, a missionary from the fishing village of Buckie in the North of Scotland, who worked for the Lord in Aruba in the Caribbean. Charles Geddes is a friend of mine. He has published his life story in his book "Love Lifted Me" – a book that has led many people to faith in the Lord Jesus. Steve said he had been greatly encouraged and uplifted in spirit by his visits to our Church on the previous Sunday and in hearing Charles Geddes speak at the meeting on the following Wednesday evening.

The next week we visited the ship with our young Malaysian student – the one who had met Steve at our house the previous Sunday.

The next day we waved goodbye to the Anastasia and also to Steve's daughter at the ship's rail. Steve was leaving the next day for America. His trip to Glasgow had done him good. I reflected that it was good for Christians to enjoy fellowship in this difficult and weary old world.

The Stormy Sea Bar

A large British research vessel often called in to Glasgow docks. When I had boarded it a couple of times in the past I had not got much encouragement. The Boarding Officer always took me into a small room at the top of the gangway as if keeping me at arm's length! However, he seemed friendly enough and would give me coffee – but always declined to take me to the mess room.

On my next visit, I decided to try and dodge the Boarding Officer and get to the mess room so that I could meet the crew. When I got to the top of the gangway, I emphasised to the man on watch duty that I would like to go to the <u>mess room</u> as I had calendars, Bibles and books for the crew. I showed him my bag with all the literature in it and allowed him to help himself, telling him everything was free. He was quite impressed and took a hand-knitted woolly hat and some football tracts. He told me all the crew were English. He then led me along a couple of passages and pointed to a door at the far end, marked "Mess Room". He returned to his watch duties and I pushed open the door. A buzz of conversation met my ears and I saw about ten men gathered round a bar drinking pints of beer. It was as if I had walked into a pub. In fact someone had painted a name above the bar in big letters "The Stormy Sea Bar"! They did not take much notice of me. One or two glanced at the name "Port Mission" on my hard hat. One man found me a seat at a small table and then asked if I would like a drink. "Yes," I said, "I'll have a Glasgow coffee!" This puzzled him a bit, but I was determined to get some attention and I thought that that was a good way of doing it. He went over to the barman and ordered a "Glasgow coffee" for the man from the mission. This also puzzled the barman and he shouted to the crowd around the bar "Has anyone heard of a Glasgow coffee?" This gave me their attention – which is what I had been seeking – and the buzz of conversation quietened. I began spreading my literature on the table and a few drifted over, their attention having been captured. Others continued to play darts and dominoes.

The barman called over to me: "We don't have any Glasgow coffee, padre!" I said, "O.K. – just make it a black coffee, one sugar!" One of the men taking a great interest in the literature was a tall man from London, who told me that he was a Christian. This was a great encouragement so I spoke out to tell everybody that all literature was free, and explained that I worked for God and pointed upwards – and to help themselves. Soon there was quite a bit of activity around the table. Many of the seamen took New Testaments and calendars and large seed sowers' texts and football tracts. The barman came over with my black coffee.

I sat for about half an hour sipping my coffee and chatting to the seamen. The tall Christian man was very happy as he clutched a handful of literature. I then produced my seamen's visitors' book and asked if anyone would like to sign it. A few did – and I packed my bag, leaving some tracts and booklets still on the table. As I made my way towards the gangway I hoped I would not run in to the Boarding Officer – but all was well. I had another ship to visit – this time with a Russian crew.

A couple of days later I noticed my seamen's visitors' book was missing and I concluded I had left it behind on the Russian ship which had now sailed away and I did not expect to see it again. It was a pity, as the book contained greetings from seamen from all over the world. However, about six months later I received the following letter:-

"Dear Mr. Laughlin,

During a recent inspection on board our research vessel laid up in Southampton, the enclosed book was found in the crew's bar. We assume that this was left on board by mistake in the vessel, following one of the visits to Glasgow earlier this year.

Yours sincerely,

Marine Personnel Manager"

So the Stormy Sea Bar turned out to be not so stormy after all! I was glad I had visited the research vessel even though I had not been too keen to do so at the beginning. After that experience, I missed no opportunity to board any ship that was berthed when I visited the docks in Glasgow.

The Superstitious Seamen!

It is said that there are 30,000 ships sailing on the oceans of the world, with over one million seamen as crew. A seaman's job is said to be one of the most dangerous jobs in the world. Ships go missing every week. They sink in heavy storms or are hit by freak waves, or they just disappear without trace – perhaps due to cyclones, hurricanes or tidal waves – or even pirates!

Seamen have told me of strange happenings at sea during terrifying storms. Many ships have on the wall of their mess room the well-known poster of an old sailing ship on a stormy sea with the steering wheel fixed on the open deck. In the poster the steers-man is lashed to the steering-wheel, guiding the ship through the storm, and hovering over his shoulders with his arms around him is the figure of an angel. Below the picture are the words "My Guardian Angel".

I boarded a ship that had come in to dock after a particularly stormy spell of weather. One seaman thought I was a Roman Catholic Priest and, as I was leaving the ship, he said "Father, when you come back to see us tomorrow please bring with you some Holy Water to bless our ship." I said to him, not wanting to hurt his feelings, "I am sorry I don't have any Holy Water but I will pray for a safe journey for your ship."

Another seaman from Portugal gave me a graphic account of seeing the Virgin Mary walking on the waves in front of his ship – guiding the ship on a very stormy night. He was very sincere about what he saw. I told him to read some of the leaflets I had left in the ship's mess room and trust the Saviour, Jesus Christ, to help him through the storm.

I quoted the old hymn:

> What a Friend we have in Jesus,
> All our sins and griefs to bear,
> What a privilege to carry
> Everything to God in prayer.

The Tall American

One of the first ships I boarded, at the beginning of my work for the Lord at the docks, was an American ship. I was just "feeling my way" and and learning as I went along.

The security "man" at the top of the gangway was a security woman - who, after pinning a visitor's label on my jacket, summoned a crew member to take me to the mess room. The moment I entered the mess room I was certain no one could be in any doubt as to the nationality of the crew of this ship! There was evidence everywhere of the American way of life - coffee machines, chocolate bar dispensers and soda fountains. Some of the crew sat relaxing on easy chairs.

I started to explain who I was…to make it clear, I said, "I am not a Mormon". And to further clarify, I added "And I am not a Jehovah's Witness". At this point, a very tall American rose to his feet and said, "Pardon me, sir, I am a Jehovah's Witness!" He looked about 7 ft. tall!

Immediately, I held out my hand to him and said, "Sorry, young man, no offence meant! I am really pleased to meet you – and may God bless you!" I dug my hand into my bag and drew out one of the best woolly hats I had, specially knitted for seamen, and offered it to him. He smilingly accepted.

I set out the contents of my bag on the table in the mess room and told the crew to help themselves. I also gave out an invitation to our gospel service on the forthcoming Sunday. My tall friend did not come, but some did, and many other Americans came to our church over the years, and for this I thank God. Men and women from many countries and from unknown islands have been offered the great privilege of hearing the gospel of Jesus Christ, and of reading His Word, the Bible. Perhaps five or six hundred seamen and women have come willingly through the doors of the old Gospel Hall in the Govan district of Glasgow, including: Russian skinheads, gentle Pacific Islanders, happy Filipinos, solemn Poles. They all came because they were attracted by the Christian faith. Even some seamen who could not understand the English language very well still came and listened attentively to the Christian message of the gospel.

And the wonder of it all is that there was not a dissenting voice among them. In all my years as Seamen's Christian Visitor there was never any walk-out by any of these dear foreign seamen during a church service. Looking back now in my old age, I sometimes wonder if it was real – then I knew in my heart that it was all the Lord's doing. It is marvellous that there is nothing too hard for the Lord.

To God be the Glory
Great things He has done.

The Turks

The crew were all from Turkey. Some people in the UK may think the Turkish people are uninterested in Christian literature – but not so. I have been on several Turkish ships and have found them most welcoming and friendly and showing a great interest in the Christian literature I display. I urge them, as I do on all ships, to take extra literature for their friends and relations back home.

I discovered one man on this ship was a Christian. He invited me to see his cabin. It was like a Christian bookshop with posters and pictures pinned to the walls. There was a large poster of the Lord's Supper, and two large Seed Sowers' texts that I had given him, along with a Christian calendar, and various other tracts and pictures. Lying on his bedside table was a large Bible and a New Testament too! It was good to see his enthusiasm for the Christian faith in a country where there are very few Christians. He was the only Christian on board this ship. I encouraged him and told him "God honours those who honour Him."

Later on, the Chief Officer gave me an invitation to come with the ship to Turkey, via Egypt, but I had to decline. It is possible that they wanted to learn more of Christianity and, if I had been a young man, I would, I am sure, have jumped at the chance.

The Wrong Door

When I board a ship, after I have identified myself, I always ask to be taken to the mess room. I am usually taken there by the seaman on watch at the top of the gangway. By asking for the mess room, I know I will meet some of the crew. If the mess room is unoccupied, there are always seamen in the adjoining galley and sometimes, if it is a big ship, in the recreation room.

When I leave the ship, bidding the crew goodbye and wishing them a safe and calm journey with God's blessing, I occasionally lose my way – should I turn left or right, or is it through this door or that, or should I go upstairs or down?

On one occasion, when taking leave of a large merchant vessel, I found myself looking uncertainly at a door that I thought would lead to the main deck and, ultimately, the gangway. I hesitantly opened the door and to my surprise discovered myself looking at two bunk beds with two girls in them – one girl lying reading and the other was just relaxing. The one who was reading gave me a puzzled look and the one who was relaxing sat up. I don't know who was the most startled – them or me. I quickly said, "I'm sorry. I think I'm lost!" And one of them said, in broken English, "What place this we are in?" (Some crews don't know the port they are in, especially if the ship is in port for a very short stay.) I said, "Glasgow, in Scotland." I decided not to linger and quickly took a step backwards and went out to look for the gangway once more!

The Man from Luton

As I approached the ship berthed at King George V Dock, I observed that she was carrying machinery from a large engineering company to the Far East. I spoke to a docker and he told me an ambulance had recently called at the ship and had taken a man to the local hospital. The docker thought he was one of the crew.

I immediately drove to the local Southern General Hospital and made enquiries. The seaman was in the High Dependency Unit. The nurse told me he had had a serious heart attack while the ship was at sea. If I returned to the hospital in a day or two, the nurse said, I would get in to see him. He was as Englishman.

Two days later, I was allowed in to see him. I introduced myself and he seemed glad to see me. He was a nice man. He came from Luton, in the south of England. I visited him a good number of times and, gradually, he improved and was soon able to sit up in a chair at the side of his bed in his dressing gown.

One day he told me he was going home to Luton. The hospital had booked a flight for him the following day. He told me he was grateful for my visits and for the New Testament and Daily Bread booklets I had given to him. I bade him good-bye and wished him God's blessing for the future.

A few days later I was visiting a church friend, again at the Southern General Hospital, and found myself walking down a long hospital corridor with wards on either side. I happened to glance in at one of the wards as I was passing and, there, sitting on a chair at the side of his bed was a man very like my friend from Luton. I walked on a bit and then paused, "Was it really him I saw just now?" I said to myself - and then shook my head "Of course not – he will be home in Luton by now!" However, to make sure, I retraced my steps for a better look. The man was dressed in a suit. I had never seen my friend dressed in a suit before! I edged closer. He smiled. "Are you the seaman from Luton?" I asked. "That's me all right, Sam!" he said. Then he told me his story. A nurse had gone with him to the airport and, when she tried to check-in the man in the wheelchair, a member of staff asked her what the trouble was. When she explained her patient was recovering from a heart attack, she was told that the rules said that anyone who had recently had a heart attack was not permitted to fly.

"So here I am, booked on a train for Luton, and waiting patiently." A couple of days later I called in again at the hospital to make sure all was well, and a nurse confirmed that my friend had arrived safely in Luton and was now in hospital there. I breathed a sigh of relief!

"The Short Strand"

"The Short Strand" lay for two weeks in the dock basin before I decided to visit her - mainly because she was in No. 10 Berth, the farthest-away berth in the entire King George V Dock.

"The Short Strand" was not really a ship; she was a giant barge constructed for salvage work and dredging. When I finally arrived at the barge, I saw right away that it was a difficult ship to board because of its construction. It had no gangway – you just stepped from the quayside on to the barge (being careful not to fall down the space between barge and quayside into the river!); you then descended ladders into the depth of the ship until you reached the level of the cabins below. It was like descending a submarine – everything was below the water level. I was anxious not to take chances and took great care boarding the barge.

Some days it was almost impossible to board because, depending on the tide, the barge was not always level with the quayside making it too dangerous to jump aboard. There was a rope ladder which I tried to use one day to lower myself on to the deck but it was too difficult for me.

You might say, "Why bother trying to board a barge like that – it had only five of a crew anyway!" But there was a man on board The Short Strand that I had a great interest in. I had met him once before. He was the Captain and his name was Fergus. He came from the Western Isles of Scotland. Fergus was about 45, a very jolly man, with a good sense of humour. When I called on him, he remembered me and greeted me in his lilting voice, "Ah,

Sam, how is my good Glasgow friend today?" I liked Fergus – but was concerned that he was too fond of the drink!

On another visit, around Christmas-time - I found Fergus and a member of the crew seated in a small cabin, drinking. I gave them the bag of goodies I give to all seamen at Christmas. Fergus thanked me and, glancing into the bag, he gave a big laugh, and said, "No whisky, Sam!" "No, Fergus," I said, "only lemonade!" Most of the crew had gone home for the Christmas and New Year holidays. There was no one else on that huge barge that night, apart from the Captain Fergus and his mate - and the surrounding dockland was deserted. It was very gloomy and quiet. The few cabins "down below" were very dark and without portholes - and they were the smallest cabins I had ever seen. Such was the place where I found Fergus and his mate that day. You could hear the sound of the water lapping against the side of the barge as Fergus poured beer into the tumblers. When he saw me, he shouted a welcome in his lilting highland voice - although his words were a bit slurred! He wanted to talk about his home. He told me that Scotland was a beautiful place but one of great contrasts.

Many people knew that the Christian way was the right way but they could not break free from the curse of drink.

We talked of the great Christian revival of the nineteen fifties that swept over the Western Isles – and about the dangerous life at sea – but Fergus laughed everything off. He refused to take anything seriously. He knew it all – and laughed.

I tried to get him to come to our Gospel Meeting on the following Sunday evening – but, no, he said, it was not for him, and to prove that his mind had moved to other things, he broke into a song. I finally left them in this dark dungeon of a place with not a sound or soul for miles around. New Year to a Scotsman is a big thing but unfortunately, for some, strong drink is an even bigger thing. He shook hands as he saw me off the barge. As I walked to my car, he shouted after me, "Sam, Sam – a Happy New Year!" and as I drove away, I could hear following me the strains of "Auld Lang Syne" drunkenly sung. I had a tear in my eye and a lump in my throat as I drove home. Could I have done more? I felt inadequate to the task. What a wasted life.

I visited Fergus regularly until, one day, I found that the big flat barge had sailed away. What can we do with a man like Fergus who seems to know it all – except to know the Saviour.

For a long time I had hoped Fergus would bring his barge back to Glasgow. I wondered if he still had the Christian calendar I had given him, stuck up on the wall of his cabin. Did he read the Seed Sowers' text of John 3:16 I gave him? Maybe, some dark stormy night at sea, he will look up this verse in the New Testament I gave him as a personal gift. Only God knows where he is now but I pray for him still.

A Warm Italian Welcome

As I drove into Glasgow Docks I saw a large ship in Berth No. 6. It turned out to be an Italian ship. This was the first time that a ship from Italy had been in Glasgow in my time. I wondered how I would be received.

I need not have worried. The all-Italian crew were very happy to see me and welcomed me on board. They were all very keen to take plenty of the literature I had available. They took extra of nearly everything – calendars for the following year (it was the month of November) Seed Sowers' texts, etc. for their families – wives and children, fathers and mothers, sisters and brothers. I also had a supply of woolly hats and everyone wanted one! I must have given out a couple of dozen! Even the Captain took a woolly hat.

They all talked and asked questions, but openly and without hostility. It was a very happy visit. I saw the crew at the beginning of the week and was only able to board the ship twice before it sailed for her next port on the Thursday. It would have been grand to take them to the Gospel Meeting on Sunday. I am sure they would have been willing to come. They were an enthusiastic and happy crew.

They gave me biscuits, and coffee in a very dainty little coffee cup which they kept refilling – black without sugar or milk.

It was a lovely new ship and very well furnished. There were curtains on the portholes and pictures on the walls. Who attended to these things I wondered? And then, two ladies appeared. They shook hands with me and brought more coffee and two pieces of cake. They wanted me to stay for lunch, but I had other ships to visit. I was sorry to see the ship leave after only two days in dock. I wished I had got to know them better before I said "Arrivederci"!

The Glory C

The Glory C was a big ship, more than 20,000 tonnes, with a crew of Filipinos, Russians and Romanians. The young Filipino Captain was a born-again Christian. I gave him a new King James Bible to be kept permanently on the ship. The Chief Engineer was also a Christian. He held a regular Bible study in his cabin for any of the crew that desired to attend. I gave him several Emmaus Bible Courses to help them in their studies. Many of the crew of this ship professed to be Christian.

They invited me to help them hold a special Bible Study in the mess room the next day. I told them I would be happy to help. I asked my good friend in the church, Bert Gamble, to help too and he agreed. The next day we arrived on board and there was a good crowd of about 20 seamen waiting. We made sure everyone had a Bible. For the next hour we read the Bible and they asked many questions. When we were leaving, the Chief Officer asked us to come back the next day for dinner in the mess room. This we did, and enjoyed a happy time with our friends.

There is a lot to encourage in a spiritual way among the people from the Philippines. They are a friendly, open, people and they love to sing the old hymns and choruses. The Chief Engineer was a lovely singer. He told me he was going to do the same as I do for the Lord among the ships that come in to the large port of Manila. As well as the Bible Courses, I gave him a hundred Seed Sowers' texts along with other literature to help him get started. For the singing in his cabin during the Bible Studies he had made up song sheets with all the well known hymns and choruses written on them and pinned each song sheet on to a long pole, rolling over one at a time. All the old favourites were there - written in both Tagalog and English.

Sadly the following year, the ship was sold to a Chinese shipping company and when that happened they gave me the roll of hymns and choruses – which I often use in my house when the seamen come to us for supper after the gospel meeting. The sale of the ship to the Chinese company went ahead so suddenly that the Chinese crew arrived to take over the ship before the existing crew of Russians, Filipinos and Romanians had left the ship! This gave me the opportunity to give the Chinese Captain a King James Bible to be used by the crew and kept on board ship. The new Chinese Captain was a very nice man, and invited me to dinner.

The ship *The Glory C* had been a regular visitor to Glasgow and I missed the ship and its crew. I had made many friends on that ship and had given out Christian literature over many years.

The Flying Phantom Tragedy

I received word from Stephen, my contact in Belfast, that there was a large ship the "Red Jasmine" due in to Glasgow the following day. The next day turned out to be a foggy, wet, miserable December day. I was told that the "Red Jasmine" (40,000 tonnes) would not be berthing until about six o'clock because of the fog – so I did not wait.

The next day, I was shocked to read the newspaper headline "Tug Goes Down in the Clyde". It seems the "Red Jasmine" was being towed up river to the docks by three tugs when, just before six o'clock, and only about two miles from her berthing point, one of the leading tugs, "The Flying Phantom" suddenly capsized and four of the crew were pitched into the freezing river. The tug apparently overturned when negotiating one of the many bends on this narrow river. Three men died almost immediately but one man was rescued and survived. It was a surprise to everybody because thousands of ships have come up and down the river in the past years and nothing like this has happened before.

This tug went down only twenty yards from the shore and only a couple of miles from the dock where I was waiting to board the "Red Jasmine". My heart went out to the families of the men who died so suddenly. It is indeed a violent and dangerous world we live in, especially so if you are a seaman.

It reminded me of the old saying "You are heading in the right direction when you walk with God."

I never really heard or read exactly what happened on that foggy evening on that bendy old River Clyde. I assume that one of the tow ropes slackened off while the ship was going round a bend in the river and got underneath the tug and suddenly, when the winch tightened the rope as it went into the straight, over it went. As far as I know, there was no alarm given. It was half an hour later, when the ship was docking, that they discovered that the tug was missing. Certainly, the heavy fog contributed to the tragedy.

The Drunken Sailor

While on holiday in Northern Ireland, I met a man who told me the story of his father, Jack McLean. Jack McLean's life was changed through contact with a Port Missionary who came on board his ship in Holyhead, in England, in 1928. In 1905, at the age of 15, Jack McLean left home and sailed out of Larne Harbour on a small ship owned by Murray of Maidens, Ayrshire. Thus began his sea-going life.

After 7 years at sea in 1912 he became a gun-runner, bringing thousands of rifles to Larne for the loyalists of Northern Ireland during those strife-torn days. He was well paid in gold sovereigns for this dangerous job, but the money was soon spent on whiskey as soon as he got ashore.

Jack joined the Royal Navy at the beginning of WW1 and was placed in trawlers to do minesweeping. After four years' service he was invalided out with a drink-related disease. This only led him on to drink even more to try to forget his troubles – but sadly found that drink never cures troubles. He was deep into difficulties and debt, a homeless vagabond.

On a visit home to Larne, he met a local girl and got married. Why she married him is a mystery, but marry him she did! He thanked God for her ever afterwards for she stood by him and he began to see what a good a wife he had. She never lost heart but struggled on to bring up the children in adverse conditions.

In 1925, Jack got a job in the Larne and Stranraer Mail Steamer. In 1928, his ship was in port at Holyhead for a general survey.

While there, the Port Missionary, Mr. West, and his wife came aboard. They held a short service in the mess room on the first Sunday afternoon. The next day Jack was invited to the Sailors' Rest where a few simple games like dominoes and darts were arranged. Jack enjoyed those evenings. It was a better way of passing the time than wandering aimlessly through the streets and propping up the pub bars.

The evenings would generally end with Mr. West reading from the Bible and giving a short sermon. It was at the Sailors' Rest that Jack heard the good news of the gospel for the first time. Mr. West told the seamen how God sent His Son Jesus into the world to die on an old rugged cross to save sinners, and he said they were all sinners – preacher and hearers alike. He quoted verses from the Bible which said that Jesus came into the world to seek and to save the lost. Jack McLean thought over his life and began to realise that he indeed was a sinner, and a lost one at that. Mr. West often quoted from the Bible John Chapter 3, verse 16:

For God so loved the world that He gave his only begotten Son
that whosoever believes in Him should not perish
but have everlasting life.

And so it happened that one night in the little partitioned room in the Sailors' Rest, Jack McLean accepted the Lord Jesus Christ as his own and personal Saviour – from the power of Satan to the power of God. What a change! When he got on board again, there were those who could not believe that the life of the drunken seaman could be so changed.

When he got home to Larne he told his wife all about it. She marvelled at the change and gave her heart also to the Lord Jesus and trusted Him for her future and hope in Heaven.

In 1933, Jack got a job with the Port of Larne Authority as a Ship Inspector with the Ministry of Agriculture. He told other seamen about his Saviour, the great Saviour of men and women. He distributed Christian literature too, telling of the Saviour who saves to the very uttermost all who come to Him and accept His offer of forgiveness.

Jack McLean often visited Mr. West in remembrance of that great day when he sailed into Holyhead and found the Lord Jesus.

The Deo Volente

The ship, Deo Volente, was owned and run by a Dutch Christian family and was the only Christian-owned ship I ever encountered. It was the joint owners' newest ship, less than one year old; a really beautiful ship, built to the highest standards.

It was berthed in No. 10 Berth, the furthest away berth in the dock, about two miles from the dock entrance and security gate. When I reached the berth, I parked my car on the quayside in front of the ship and got out to have a closer look at what was going on. It was an interesting sight - they were unloading giant wind turbines.

I noticed a young woman walking on the open deck with a little woolly poodle dog on the lead. There was no gangway owing to the type of cargo they were discharging. I shouted that I wished to come aboard. Beckoning me, she smiled and said "I will show you" and unchained a gate on the ship's rail. She was very interested when I explained I was Seamen's Christian Visitor to Glasgow Docks. Although Dutch, she spoke perfect English and told me that it would soon be the afternoon break for the crew. I was taken into a lounge and she provided me with coffee and biscuits. Soon the officers and crew drifted in from work and she introduced me to her husband, Berend Hartman, who was the ship's Captain. The officers and crew consisted of Dutch seamen and Filipinos. The young woman, told me that her name was Ineke. The little poodle dog was Dutch too – and his name was Pluto!

During my conversation with the Captain I discovered that

the ship would, for the duration of their contract, be coming from Denmark to Glasgow every second weekend with a cargo of wind turbines. I visited the ship whenever she docked in Glasgow - and so began a long association with the Deo Volente which continues even to the present day.

The ship's crew did not work on a Sunday and had their own church service but they came to our gospel meeting on the Sunday evenings. Sometimes the whole crew of about twelve or thirteen came along – (Pluto-the-poodle remained behind to guard the ship!). They all sat at the one table during meals and gave thanks to God for the food provided.

Before the Deo Volente's contract ended, my wife and I were invited to take a short voyage to Denmark and back to Glasgow. I would have loved a trip on this wonderful ship but, sadly, health problems prevented me.

We still keep in touch by email with this lovely couple. News of the birth of their son Theodore gave us much pleasure.

The Dentist

It was a Greek ship. The Captain of the ship, and the officers were of Greek nationality, but the crew was mainly composed of Filipinos. Eight of them came to the gospel meeting. Sam Hanlon, a former missionary from Honduras, was the speaker. I welcomed them all at my house afterwards and we sang some of the old gospel hymns; one man played the guitar very well.

I visited the ship again during the week and one man, an officer, said he had severe toothache and could I help him as it was driving him crazy. I told him I would take him to a dentist. We visited a local dentist in Cardonald but the receptionist said we would have to wait in a queue as they were busy - and they would charge for any treatment done.

I did not think this was suitable, so I suggested taking him to the Dental Hospital, where patients could be seen immediately if they were suffering pain. Treatment was normally free of charge, but would be done by students under the supervision of a qualified dentist. He was quite happy about this and we made for Sauchiehall Street where the Dental Hospital was located. When we spoke to the receptionist, she said the seaman would get priority as his ship was sailing the next day. I waited for him and, after half an hour, he appeared holding his jaw. He told me a young girl had done all the work. She had given him a jag and had pulled out a large back tooth - which she gave him as a souvenir of Glasgow to show to his shipmates! He showed the tooth to me and I told him it was the biggest tooth I had ever seen! The Captain would probably tie a rope to it and use it as a spare anchor in rough weather!

As we parted that day, I told him that by God's provision, he had received a Bible, clothing, a woolly hat, a calendar and, now, free dental treatment. The seaman was very happy and said "God very good to poor Greek seaman!"

When the ship left the next day a very happy Greek officer had a big smile for everyone.

Unknown Destination!

I have had some narrow escapes while on board ship! For example, I would be unaware, for the moment, that the crew which had made me so welcome on board had all deserted the mess room. I would begin to pack my bag and then I would suddenly realise that the ship was preparing to set sail! Quickly glancing out of the porthole I would discover that the pilot was already on board and the crew were pulling up the gangway! At the last minute I would scramble ashore.

It happens like this: I have been in the mess room for maybe half an hour with all my literature spread out on the table waiting on the crew to look in – but often they are all out working. Many come to look, lifting Christian literature and Seed Sowers' texts, and then go back to work. I wait on…to see if any more of the crew is coming then I finally pack my bag - not knowing the crew are pulling up the gangway and casting off the ropes and preparing to set sail! The crew usually get a big surprise when I come out shouting "Hold on! Hold on!" And some, with good humour, laugh and shout "Hurry, hurry, Mr. Sam!"

On some of my visits, I wondered as I sat in the mess room of a ship with the crew now away back to work after lunch if it would suddenly sail away while I was still on board. It used to conjure up in my mind all sorts of ideas of what could happen if I was caught out and had to sail with a ship.

Well, it did happen in a sort of a way when I boarded a ship with a crew from Estonia. As I walked down a passage towards the mess room several seamen passed me by. I tried to speak to them but they seemed to be in a bit of a hurry and did not know much English – and the mess room was empty; the lunch hour was over and I assumed that what I saw was the crew going back to their work – painting and repairing and helping with unloading the cargo. I sat at a table sorting out my Bibles and books, etc. and waited about 15 minutes - but no one appeared, so I decided to pack up and go. I moved out to the open deck towards the gangway - but there was no gangway there! And the ship was moving!

I ran towards the ship's rail; by this time the ship had drawn out from the quay and was about five feet away from the quay and moving quite fast. My first reaction was to throw my bag of literature on to the quay and jump from the rail but then I pulled up and said to myself "Don't panic!" To jump might have been all right if the level of the quay had been below the level of the rail of the ship and so I would have been jumping downwards but in fact the quay was at least 12 inches above the level of the ship's rail which meant I would have had to jump up and forward at the same time. This would be rather risky. I might be able to land on the quay all right but it was more than likely that I would stagger backwards and receive an early bath in the River Clyde!

So I quickly calmed down, laid my bag against the bulk head, sat down on top of it and contemplated my position! Where would my journey end - Estonia, Russia, or maybe Amsterdam, or perhaps just Greenock? Then suddenly I noticed the ship was slowing down considerably. Maybe someone had remembered I might still be on the ship. It slowly pulled in to another berth further down the river. Soon the gangway was back in position. I lifted my bag, walked down the gangway and found my feet on dry land again! No one spoke to me and no explanation was given. I said goodbye to those leaning on the rail and made my way back to King George V Dock and my car. Still, I was a bit disappointed I had not completed my mystery tour!

But I believe it was really another instance of the Lord taking care of His own.

Too Much For Me

I thought at first, going by its name, that it was a British ship I had boarded, but, no, it had an all-Russian crew.

A man with a beard welcomed me aboard and we went to a very small mess room. It was here I intended to lay out my Christian literature for the crew.

When I entered the mess room, there was a very big, heavy, man sitting watching the television. He did not look like a seaman; he never looked at me all the time I was there, and he was only an arm's length from me. If it had been before the break-up of the USSR, I would have thought he was a political man, a sort of a KGB spy.

However, if the big man ignored me, the man with the beard certainly made up for it! He asked me if I would like something to eat. I said, "Just a coffee will do, please." I was not hungry but it was very cold outside and a cup of coffee would soon heat me up. All I wanted was a cup of black coffee with one spoonful of sugar. I am not a very big eater, and I didn't really want to eat off the seamen. So I told the man, "Just a coffee."

On board any ship, when seamen begin to lay food down in front of me, I just don't have the heart to tell them I don't want it. Indeed, to refuse would sometimes cause offence. If offered food, and it is near lunch time, I will say: "Yes, some soup and a little rice." I like rice, and on the ships with Asians in the crew, there is usually a large pot of boiled rice sitting on a table, and everyone helps themselves. But on this ship, the Russian man with the beard was determined to ply me with all kinds of food and plenty of it. Maybe he could not understand me, for he was not a good speaker of English, and that would be why he kept piling up the food in front of me. Or maybe he thought I was under-nourished because, sitting beside the big, heavy, man, I probably looked under-nourished! Then the cook emerged with a large plate of bread and biscuits and a plate of various types of ham. Taking one of the slices of bread, and laying it on the flat of his hand, he said "I show you!" He then proceeded to spread on it slices of butter about half an inch thick and piled the ham on top. He then repeated the procedure with another slice of bread, and piled on more ham, tomatoes and various other vegetables until the sandwich was at least three inches thick! Then the bearded man appeared on the scene again, this time with plates of tinned fruit and more coffee. Finally, as I was preparing to leave, he gave me a bag of apples and oranges and three jars of jam (made, appropriately, in Hungary!) and put them all in my bag along with cans of coca cola.

As for the food, I could hardly look at it, never mind eat it, but I did my very best. While all this was going on, the big man never uttered a word.

I was glad to get off that ship I can tell you!

What?

It was a stormy winter afternoon of howling wind and rain – but I was happy as I approached this ship because I could see it was a Scottish ship registered in Lerwick, the main town of the Shetland Isles, off the northern coast of Scotland.

It is changed days at the docks from what it used to be when many Scottish ships came into Glasgow. When I got out of my car and had a closer look at the ship I noticed there was no gangway – which meant there was little chance of going on board. I was getting too old to jump and grab the rail and climb on to the main deck as many of the seamen do when their ship is in dock. Sometimes they don't bother putting on a gangway if the ship is only going to be in dock for a short time. Another thing I noticed was that there was a seaman doing some work on the open deck. It was helpful someone was there, but with no gangway on the ship we would have to communicate by shouting across to each other. To make matters worse, there was a strong wind blowing and I did not want to stand too near the edge of the quay in case I got caught in a gust of wind and was blown into the river.

To be frank, I would not have bothered about this ship on such a bad day but I knew a man who was born and brought up in Shetland and thought that this seaman may know him.

I called out to him, "Are you from Shetland?" He did not pay any attention, or he may not have heard me because of the wind and the rain. I shouted again, louder, "Are you from Shetland? Do you know a man called Mr. Watt?" He lifted his head and called back "What?" I answered, "Yes! Yes! Mr. Watt!" He shouted back "What?" I called back as loudly as I could, "Yes, Mr. Watt!" He came a bit closer and shouted again "What?" I changed tack and pointed to him, "You from Shetland?" "Me from Poland," he replied. I got such a surprise I shouted "What?" He replied, "All crew from Poland!"

I moved back to my car. I had had enough. I gave him a wave and shouted "Goodbye!" He shouted in reply, "What?" and I jumped into my car. And then I had an afterthought – I got out of the car again and opened the boot and took a woolly hat out of my bag, along with two Polish New Testaments. I wrapped the New Testaments inside the woolly hat to keep it from blowing away in the wind and lobbed the hat and the New Testaments on to the deck of the ship. I watched as he lifted the bundle. He put on the woolly hat and put the New Testaments into his pocket. Satisfied at last, I drove off.

As I drove past the Security Man at the gatehouse he slid open his window and shouted, "What a day!" I said, "What?" He repeated, "What a day!" I drove on.

Christmas Day

One Christmas Day, I was quite surprised to find seven ships berthed at King George V Dock. It was very early in the morning and the place was deserted – not a soul stirred. I knew I wouldn't be able to stay too long as we had arranged to visit our Ethiopian friend, Tesfaye, and his family, for Christmas dinner, and we had to make the 20 mile journey to his home in Kilmarnock; not only that, I didn't have enough goodies to go round seven ships!

The first two ships I boarded had Russian and Polish crews. They were all happy to see me, and I soon ran out of mince pies, chocolate ginger biscuits, and carmel wafers (a great favourite)! The Poles had a decorated Christmas tree in their mess room. The Russians also had decorations up. The Russians wanted me to stay for dinner but I told them my wife and I had arranged to go to friends – but the Chief Officer said they had a great Cordon Bleu cook - an old Russian Navy man – so I agreed to take soup only, and they were happy. I was tempted to take a main course also, but had I done so I would not have been able to eat the dinner our Ethiopian friends in Kilmarnock had so lovingly prepared.

Fifteen years previously my wife, Wilma, and I had befriended Tesfaye, a young man from Ethiopia. He was the first of many international students from all over the world in whom my wife and I had taken an interest when they arrived to study at one of Glasgow's three universities.

He is a graduate in economics. After settling in Scotland, he got a job as a lecturer in an Ayrshire College. Now in a promoted post at the same college, he still lives happily in Scotland today with his wife and daughter and two boys.

Before I left the ships I visited, I gave each seaman a bag containing a woolly hat, a New Testament, a Christmas card, a Christmas tract, and a Seed Sower's poster – and left them happy.

I wondered if there were any Filipinos in the other five ships I had been unable to visit. One Christmas past, a Filipino crew had had great fun roasting a pig over a special spit they had put up – they gave me a taste of the freshly roasted pork and it was delicious!

I had distributed all my Christmas gifts and I had to go. I would go back to the ships on Boxing Day all being well.

Gangways!

The coaster was from the North of Scotland, registered in Lerwick in the Shetland Isles. As I drew closer to the ship, I noticed they had not bothered to put on a gangway. Perhaps they were only going to be a short time in Glasgow, I thought. Many of the smaller ships neglect to put up a gangway and the crew just jump on and off the ship as they please – but it can be dangerous for people not used to it.

I remember one ship where they had a rope ladder hanging from the deck, which they used for going on and off the ship at low tide. A perpendicular rope ladder is quite a difficult thing to climb if one is not used to climbing mountains! I had a go at it on this ship, and I can tell you it took me all my strength to get on to that deck! It was not so bad coming down, but I never ventured up a rope ladder again.

Some time later on another ship they had used an ordinary wooden ladder to bridge the gap from the quay to the ship. It was also a very dodgy climb as the ladder was at a slope from the quay to the deck and had no handrail on either side. I had to climb up on my hands and knees until I reached the deck of the ship. One wobble and I would have been thrown into the river. Climbing down the ladder from the ship to the quay was even worse! I never did anything like that again either.

I noticed that the coaster was a British-registered ship with a large thistle emblem on the funnel. "Ah," I thought, "A good old Scottish ship at last."

I hailed a sailor working on deck "Hello, are you from the Shetlands?" He looked a bit puzzled, so I called again – this time louder "Are you from the Shetlands?" He shouted back "Me from Poland." I said "Are all the crew from Poland?" He answered, "All crew from Poland." My heart sank. What has happened to the great British Merchant Fleet – with the traditional Scottish Chief Engineer and seamen from the highlands and islands of Scotland who had sailed the world's oceans for hundreds of years? Where were all those famous shipping lines that we, as boys who lived near the docks in Glasgow, had got to know – the White Star Line, the Clan Line, the Burns & Laird Line, the Ben Line, the Donaldson Line, the Anchor Line, and many, many more. The absence of a gangway on the coaster meant that I could not risk the high jump to get aboard. Goodbye coaster - and "God bless the crew" I called out as I left them.

On big ships of about 15,000 tonnes and over, the gangways always run from the quay, hugging the side of the ship straight up to the deck. Such gangways are worked electronically by the watchman who stands on the deck. I often have had to stand on the quay and shout to get his attention, because the gangway is always drawn up about 6 ft. from the quay for security reasons. With hand-signals I would tell him to lower the gangway until I could step on to it from the quay.

Then begins the long climb to the top – some of these gangways seem to be about a mile long, especially when I am carrying my bag of literature, and perhaps a bag of clothes, woolly hats and shoes. Often I had to make two journeys. Sometimes I would call up to the watchman to come down and help me to carry my bags. Sometimes, if it was a lazy watchman, he would pretend not to understand, assuming a puzzled expression and calling "No understand!" - but I usually won the day by moving my bag up and down and signalling him again to come and help me.

On one ship at Christmas-time, the watchman was a very nice Filipino and he carried everything for me right into the mess room. As a reward, I gave him one of the bags of goodies I had made up for Christmas presents for each seaman on Christmas morning. He looked inside the bag before he went back to his post at the top of the gangway and he was so delighted when he saw what it contained that he kept shaking my hand and saying "You not Mr. Sam, you Santa Claus!"

Fyne Spirit

The old River Clyde tug called *Cockchafer* had been lying at King George V Docks for the last couple of years, rusting away to nothing. A German company finally bought it and, in one year, transformed it into a beautiful tourist ship. It will be based in Loch Fyne, sailing out of Inverary, and will take tourists on trips to the surrounding area.

Several workers have been employed to work on the ship, mostly from Poland, but also a man from St. Vincent, an island in the Caribbean, and a man from the Philippines. The man from St. Vincent, Glenroy Higgins, was a fine Christian man with a good knowledge of scripture. He came with me to the Gospel Meeting several times. He has three children in St. Vincent and each of their names is prefixed by the word "Glen". He was convinced that there was some Scottish influence in his name from many centuries ago – and there may be some truth in this.

The ship has since left Glasgow and will no doubt now be plying its trade at Inverary - and Glenroy has returned to his island home in St. Vincent.

When talking with Glenroy one day about the unusual Christian names, all beginning with "Glen" he has given his children, I suggested to him that if he had another addition to the family, a baby boy, he should call him Glenelg. He asked me "Why Glenelg?" I explained that Glenelg is the name of a small village in the Highlands of Scotland and its name is unique among village names because it is spelt the same way backwards and forwards! Glenroy thought this was very amusing, and a great example of a real Scottish name!

As far as I know, "Glenelg" has not yet made his appearance; perhaps he never will! But it's a good name all the same!

Tuvalu and Kiribati

The South Pacific island of Tuvalu has featured prominently among the ships that came in to Glasgow in the late nineteen nineties and it always lifted my heart when I saw one of these tidy little ships sitting by the riverside as if waiting to welcome me, once they got to know me, with the greeting "Ah, Mr. Sam". Of all the seamen I have met in my visits to the ships, the good people of Tuvalu and its neighbouring island of Kiribati, come high in my estimation for gentleness and kindness and great open-hearts towards God. They have a quiet, pleasant nature, and friendliness, that appealed to me very much.

Home to about 10,500 people, Tuvalu is the third smallest country in the world, measuring only ten square miles. It was a former British colony and is still a Commonwealth member. Unfortunately, the island is no more than 15 feet above sea level because it is very low lying and because of climate change and global warming it is constantly at risk from rising sea levels and may become uninhabitable in the near future. The capital has the romantic-sounding name of "Funafuti".

I have never come away from visiting a Tuvalu or Kiribati ship without a souvenir of some kind. Many beautiful hand-made seashell necklaces have been given to me, or sometimes a T-shirt usually yellow in colour with the name Kiribati or Tuvalu printed across the front. A Kiribati man also gave me a DVD of the annual independence day celebrations - which is a delight to watch with all the island organisations on parade: schools, bands, nurses, girl guides, boy scouts, and many others - all parading in their uniforms.

The seamen, when in Glasgow, often came to the gospel meetings and afterwards to my house for supper. They were all big men, like rugby players but, when they sang for us, they sang in sweet soft tones, like the gentle giants they were. I gave them good clothing, woolly hats, and Christian literature, and they always expressed their appreciation of my visit.

Then, suddenly, their ships stopped coming in to Glasgow. I don't know why. For a couple of years they must have had a contract to call in to Glasgow regularly – and then it finished. I was sorry. I really missed them. We used to talk about the British missionary, John Williams, who for many years, at the turn of the century, visited these small islands in his little boat, telling them of the Lord Jesus and the way of salvation. They had heard of John Williams and said there was still a boat from Australia with Christians aboard who visited them to preach the gospel, and the name of the boat was the M/V John Williams, in memory of the good man who first brought the good news of the gospel of the Lord Jesus Christ to their islands many years ago.

Kiribati and Tuvalu were occupied by Japanese forces during the war. The seamen would tell of the British and Australian secret agents who were on the islands during WWII to record Japanese shipping movements in the Pacific Ocean during the four years of war with Japan. Twenty-two of the agents were caught and executed by the Japanese as spies. A memorial to these brave men was recently unveiled and the ceremony was reported in The Times of London. I managed to obtain a report of the entire ceremony. "**Island Honour** - Wellington: A memorial has been unveiled commemorating 22 coastal lookouts who were executed by the Japanese in 1942. The watchers, from Australia, Britain and New Zealand, were captured in the Pacific island of Kirkbati" *The Times, 12th November 2002.*

I still look out expectantly, when I visit King George V Dock, for a ship waiting for me again with the registration name "Funafuti" on it and a couple of the crew leaning over the rail and greeting me "Ah, Mr. Sam".

Sometimes, when a Funafuti or Kiribati ship was in the docks, I would put on the T-shirt they once gave to me with the name "Kiribati" printed across the front. "Ah, Mr. Sam," they would say, "You now good Kiribati man! You come some time to Kiribati to visit us!" I said, "I will come one day perhaps, but I am not a very good swimmer!"

Roast Lamb

This was the first all-Indian ship that I had been on. Two of the crew had promised to come to the Gospel Hall on the following Sunday – a man from Goa and a Pathan tribesman from the Khyber Pass area in the North West Frontier. The Khyber Pass was a place I was quite familiar with as I had served as a young soldier in the nearby town of Peshawar, and at a little hill station called Cherat, near the Afghan border.

The man from Goa and the man from the Khyber Pass kept their word and came with me to the Gospel Meeting. This was quite an unusual mix, I thought - an R.C. from Goa and a Muslim from the Afghan border. After the meeting, they joined with the rest of our church fellowship to visit Kirkcare, the local old folks home, where we had hymn singing, gospel preaching, and tea and cakes.

I went back to the ship on Monday and was walking down a passageway and had to dodge a dead sheep hanging from a girder. Talk about fresh meat! It still had all its wool on – so I don't think it was ready for the pot just yet! The Captain told me he was from Karachi, a city I knew well having stayed there during my time in the army. We talked about Elphinstone Street and the adjoining island of Manora – where I spent a pleasant two weeks in an army hospital recovering from a foot injury.

On the Thursday, I visited the ship for the last time, and the Captain's last words to me were "Pray for me, Mr. Sam." He looked a troubled man. I was sorry for him. He was very interested in the Christian faith. He was not happy the way he was. He needed Christ as His Saviour.

From Every Corner!

2004 was a record year as far as bringing seamen to our little church in Linthouse, Glasgow, was concerned. In that year seamen came from many countries: China, Taiwan, Romania, the Philippines, Russia, Poland, Turkey, Burma, India, Ukraine, Africa, and Iceland, to name but a few. These young men gave us no trouble. It was a joy to see them come in to the church quietly, and sit reverently listening to the speaker – many never having heard the gospel of Jesus Christ before. During my 16 years as a Seamen's Christian Visitor more than 600 seamen came to the gospel services. Sometimes only one or two came, but sometimes as many as fifteen attended (the entire crew of a ship apart from the watchman). Most of them came to my house for supper after the church service and I and other Christian friends took the seamen back to the ship by car afterwards.

Yar Zar Nay Win, a Christian sea cadet from Burma on board a Korean ship docked in Glasgow, came to two of our services and left the following message on my Visitors' Book (in his own version of English):

> "Thank you everything and, if God favours us,
> I would like you to meet you again.
> May God bless you more."
> Signed Zar Nay Win, Burma

One year later, I received notice of his death at the age of 20 in a tragic accident while his ship was in Japan. (Read about Yar Zar Nay Win in the story of *The Ship from South Korea* in this book.)

Warships

As I entered the docks today I saw a welcome change – two warships sitting serenely in the docks. I recognised by their flags that one was Norwegian and the other Dutch. I have come across warships on previous occasions. They are all part of the NATO fleet of ships and sometimes when on an exercise they gather in the large basin in King George V Dock in Glasgow before going out to the Atlantic on manoeuvres. On one occasion there were as many as ten warships crammed into the basin – all from different European countries. I have never been made very welcome on any of these ships – even when showing my dock pass – but I always put this down to "security reasons".

Because of this, I was a bit apprehensive as I approached these two foreign warships – but nevertheless I decided I would have another go – starting with the Dutch ship. I looked up to the top of the gangway and saw the gleaming source of power of the Dutch navy shining in the sunlight.

There was a group of about six smartly turned out officers on guard at the top of the gangway standing motionless, eyeing me up as I approached the gangway carrying a zipped-up bag. I may have looked rather suspicious. It was a testing time for these young men and women endeavouring to uphold the power of their country in a foreign port and among other foreign warships. I don't think I looked menacing as I approached - but THE BAG - I was half way up the gangway when I remembered the bag (it was a risk). I stopped and glanced up. Three or four of them had guns. One was a tall young lady who had what looked like a machine gun cradled in her arm. I turned back down the gangway and left my bag down against the wall of the quay shed and turned and made my way once again up the gangway. With hindsight this was a mistake and must have made me look rather suspicious. Now, as I approached the top of the gangway my old army days came back to me. I was waiting for someone to point a gun at me and shout "Halt! Who goes there?" But no, all was quiet. I joined them and pointed to my yellow hard hat and the simple words printed on it "Port Mission". I showed them my security letter from dock authority giving me permission to board ship. None of them said a word. I couldn't help looking at the tall lady in the dark blue uniform with the machine gun on her arm. I thought I saw she had her finger on the trigger and I had always been taught never to rest your finger on the trigger of a gun except when in action; at all other times the forefinger should be straight and stiff on the barrel of the gun, near to the trigger. This lady looked as if she was ready for action. I shook hands with one of the officers and asked if I could come on board the ship and perhaps go to the mess room. I also asked if I could return for my bag – which contained Christian literature for the crew. He seemed a bit taken aback. They spoke quickly together and, after a pause, the officer said he was sorry but, no, he could not allow me to come aboard today - but if I came back tomorrow morning (which was Sunday) it would be all right.

None of the others spoke. I thanked him. I was hoping the machine-gun lady would say a word. I had the feeling she was just itching to have a go at something with her tommy-gun. I moved down the gangway and at the bottom gave them a little wave. I then walked over to the wall and picked up my bag. I gave another glance upwards. They did not seem to be discussing what had taken place – they looked a bit bewildered. As I walked down the quay towards my Sierra car I felt sorry for them. They were young, and clean-cut, and doing their duty. Maybe I should have taken my bag up the gangway in the first place and presented each of them with a New Testament. With these thoughts, I decided to give the Norwegian ship a miss and move on to more familiar ground.

Yet the thought lingered and I remembered the lines from scripture

> I was hungry and you gave me food
> I was a stranger and you took me in
> . . . in as much as you have done it
> unto the least of these my brethren . . .
> You have done it to me.

Fire in the Galley

I went on board a large ship on a bitterly cold day. The seaman on watch at the top of the gangway was so well muffled up against the cold that it was difficult to see his face – but, when I got to the top of the gangway, I saw that he was a Filipino. He mumbled something to me that I could not make out. I repeated firmly "Mess room! All right for mess room?" After seeking advice by phone he took me to a room marked "Ship's Office" and said "Wait here, please."

While I waited, I took out some Christian literature from my bag and began laying it out on a small table. As I was doing so, a very loud alarm bell suddenly went off and a loud speaker repeatedly blared out "Fire in the galley; fire in the galley; fire in the galley!" To make matters worse, as the alarm bells continued to ring, and the loud speaker blared, the lights went out. I remained where I was and, after a few minutes, to my relief, the lights came back on.

However, there was still a lot going on! The crew ran back and forward putting on life jackets and wearing breathing masks. Watching, it began to dawn on me that this might be a training exercise, (timed to take place while the ship was in dock) so I followed the men down the passageway to the door that led to the open deck. There I saw the crew lowering the lifeboats – so I stopped one of the crew and asked what was going on. He said "One hour and o.k."

I went back to the Ship's Office and looked around for a life jacket. I was not sure what to do. What if this was a real emergency?"

Just at that, a man came running along the passage and glanced in at the Ship's Office. He looked as if he knew what was going on. He had on a blue boiler suit with not a mark on it and a collar and tie. I asked him if he was a crew member. He said he was not. He was a safety inspector and his job was to check fire and safety drills on ships in various ports to make sure everything was in order if an emergency should arise. He said this drill would soon be over. I thanked him and told him that I had not been aware that the drill was to take place – but in my heart I was glad I had not panicked and tried to climb in to a life boat!

After about another half an hour, the crew began to drift back to their duties and, to my relief, the bell stopped ringing. I was about to leave the ship and go back to my car when the Fire Drill Inspector came back accompanied by the Filipino Captain. He welcomed me and apologised that no one had informed me about the drill. He was a friendly man and I told him about our Church meeting the following evening. He said he would be free to come but, just in case something should turn up, he asked me to give him my phone number and he would phone me on Sunday afternoon to confirm if everything was all right. I agreed that would be fine and I said I would meet him with the car at the gangway of his ship at six o'clock on the Sunday evening. He seemed enthusiastic – but on the Sunday afternoon no phone call came.

I returned to the docks on the Tuesday afternoon but the ship was away. The foreman docker, Alex, told me the Captain spoke to him and told him he had tried to phone my home on the Sunday but he could not get through and was disappointed as he was ready to come with me to the Gospel Meeting. It was then I realised why he could not get through. I had made the mistake when I gave him my phone number of not adding on the code number 0141 for Glasgow for those phoning from a ship or from a mobile phone. I was very sorry about this but was glad to be free from the "fire in the galley" that never was.

The Pipe Smoker

Many of the seamen I have met are cigarette smokers but I have only met one seaman that smoked a pipe. He was from Ireland and had been brought up in a small village near Ballymena. He was preparing his pipe one day when I joined him in leaning over the ship's rail . . . . . and we talked. "Do you ever read books?" I asked him, as he and I stared into the river. He began filling his pipe and his actions brought back memories of my own father who also smoked a pipe.

It was no straight-forward operation. The seaman first scraped out the bowl of his pipe with a penknife, then he took a pouch from his pocket and took out a piece of black tobacco. Laying his pipe down, he began to cut thin slices from the piece of tobacco, the slices dropping in to the hollow of his hand. Putting the pouch away, he began to rub the slices of tobacco together in his hand, and when it was teased to his satisfaction, he proceeded to stuff the black tobacco into his pipe, packing it down with his thumb. Then he fished in his pocket for a box of matches. The first three matches blew out in the wind, so we moved to a more sheltered spot where, at the fourth match, his pipe began to show signs of life. His puffs of smoke got stronger and stronger and he settled down contentedly. I told him my mother often good humouredly told my father "If God meant you to smoke a pipe He would have put a chimney in your head!"

Now that he had got his pipe going, the seaman turned to me and said "Where were we? Oh yes, do I read? Well, I have read cups and sometimes a newspaper, but, no, I have never read a book! No time." He talked of the art of preparing a pipe and smoking it.

I told him of the large corner shop in Glasgow's Queen Street that specialised in products for pipe smokers. Their famous designer pipes cost a fortune. They had several brands of scented tobacco one of which was their famous Presbyterian Mixture. There were pipes of all shapes and sizes from the humble clay pipe to the famous briar. All in all it was like a tobacco museum.

We talked of the men and women who never smoked but chewed tobacco like chewing gum. I told him it was a habit my own grandfather seemed to enjoy.

When I was a boy visiting my grandfather in Northern Ireland during the long summer holidays I was always fascinated by his habit of chewing tobacco. Sitting "fornenst" the open peat fire of an evening he demonstrated how he used the open fire as a spittoon. Sometimes I would point out a target and he, being an expert shot, always got a bull's eye! One evening we were sitting round the fire with a couple of our farmyard cats stretched out enjoying the heat. My favourite cat was called Lugs, so named because he had only one ear due to a fight when a very young cat. As Lugs lay dreaming, one of my grandfather's missiles fell short of the fire and, with some force, landed on Lugs' eye! What a shock for poor Lugs! Awakened out of his dreams, he did a somersault and shot like lightning through the open door! There was much laughter, but I felt sorry for Lugs. Chewing tobacco was not a nice habit but it did not do my grandfather any harm. He lived to be one hundred years old!

Down Memory Lane

I saw this ship away on the far side of the dock basin. It looked like a coaster. I did not feel like going a mile round the dock basin for such a small ship – however, I trained my 1914 German binoculars on the ship and noticed that it was registered in Inverness. Ah, a Scottish ship at last! There was also a large thistle painted on the funnel – so I decided to go the distance and investigate.

As I came near, I saw there was a man working on the open deck. I called to him from the quayside: "Are you from Inverness?" He looked a bit puzzled, so I called him again: "You Inverness man? Where are you from?" He replied, "From Poland!" I said "All crew from Poland? He said "Yes – all crew." "Captain from Poland too?" "No," he replied. "Captain Pakistan man!

After this exchange, I climbed the gangway and asked the man to take me to the Captain. I was interested in Pakistan having spent almost four years as a young soldier in India and Pakistan and the Indian / Burmese border. The Captain was a nice man. He came from the city of Karachi – a town I knew quite well. When he heard I had been to Karachi, he was happy. We talked of Napier Barracks and Elphinstone Street, both of which he knew. I asked if he had heard of the Indian Navy Mutiny which occurred when I was a young soldier in India in 1946. In the troubled days before partition, Indian ships lay off Keamari Docks and refused to dock at their headquarters on Manora Island. Our battalion of The Black Watch was ordered to invade the island and take charge of the island headquarters - while solders of another British regiment targeted the ships. Quite soon the Indian Navy diplomatically decided to dock at Manora after all, and some of the young soldiers (myself included) got the benefit of a few days "holiday" on the sandy beaches of Manora – maintaining the peace and seeing that all was safe and secure. In those days, Karachi was a pleasant coastal city and I was surprised when the Captain told me that it was now a large city of 21 million people.

I told the Captain that I remained in India until after 1947 when India was partitioned and the new country of Pakistan was "born". My regiment later moved up to the North West Frontier near the border of Afghanistan. Names that crop up in today's news bulletins – Peshawar, Landi Kotal and The Kyber Pass – were familiar to us even then!

The Captain was interested in the literature I left for the crew. Jokingly, I asked him for a lift to Manora Island. "It has changed a lot since you were there!" he smiled.

Ed's Big Day

I first met Ed on one of the American ships that came in to Glasgow regularly; that was before the 9/11 attack on the twin towers in New York when almost 3,000 people were killed. Everything changed after that.

I became quite friendly with Ed. One day he confided that he was planning to marry a Scottish girl. He told me that he had met her in a nice hotel not far from the docks. The wedding, he said, was to take place in Paisley Abbey on a date in July. Paisley Abbey is a large and beautiful centuries-old church and is often chosen as the venue for "posh" weddings. An ideal venue for Ed's wedding! Ed always dressed very smartly. He wore a goatee beard (with a pony tail to match) – and from the first time I met him, I thought he resembled King George V.

. . . . . months flashed past and it was now the month of March and I had forgotten all about Ed. He had returned to the United States after giving me the news of his forthcoming wedding - and his ship had not berthed in Glasgow since then. However, as 9 July approached, it all suddenly came back to me: Ed was getting married soon in Paisley Abbey!

9th July dawned warm and sunny, and I suggested to my wife, Wilma, that we should pay a visit to Paisley to see Ed emerging from the Abbey with his bride. The only problem was that I did not know the exact time of the wedding. When we arrived at the Abbey it was obvious that a wedding was in progress. The Abbey doors were closed but several cars were parked in front of the Abbey, including a large wedding limousine - and a few curious on-lookers had gathered nearby. We sat on a low wall in the sunshine and waited to see what happened.

After a short time, the big doors of the Abbey opened wide and the wedding party and guests began to emerge. A piper led the procession of men in kilts and ladies in all their wedding finery and summer hats. Judging by the company, it seemed that Ed had done very well for himself! At the centre of the gathered company we soon spotted Ed himself, resplendent in kilt and sporran, with his lovely bride on his arm. He saw us waiting and beckoned us over to be introduced to his bride. She was very happy to meet us – and we her - and Ed was so delighted we had not forgotten his wedding day that he invited us to the wedding reception in a hotel on the banks of Loch Lomond! We were very glad we had not forgotten Ed's Big Day.

Newly-weds dream of golden days ahead but, in reality, no one knows with any certainty what the future holds. In good times and bad, the Christian believes that nothing can separate us from the love of God. Always, at all times, waking or sleeping, we are upheld by confidence in the unfailing love of God. Therefore, if God is for us, who can be against us? He gave His own Son to die on the cross for us all – can we not therefore trust such a God to give us everything that we need? In all things we have the victory through Jesus Christ our Lord, who by His sacrificial death has proved His love for us. (Romans 8: 31-37).

I never saw Ed again but I have often thought of him. He never accepted my invitation to our church because he always reserved Sunday evenings to see his girlfriend (now his wife). I wish him well – but every time I see a picture of King George V I think of Ed!

Every Blessing

The large ship in dock had a Croatian Captain and Croatian Officers and a Filipino crew. Its country of origin was Brazil and its cargo was animal feed. They were glad to find shelter as they had encountered some stormy weather on the long journey to Scotland.

I went on board briefly, telling the crew that I was the Port Missionary. To give them time to settle in dock, I promised to return to the ship the following day. As I was leaving, a crew member appealed to me: "Father," he said, "when you come back to our ship tomorrow, will you bring some holy water with you to bless our ship and protect us from the stormy sea?" I explained with kindness that I was not a priest, I was Mr. Sam the Port Missionary, and I did not have any holy water. But I promised to pray to our Heavenly Father to protect the ship from the stormy sea. He thanked me very much.

I was made very welcome on my return visit. As a result, four crew members, all Filipinos, attended our Gospel Service on the following Sunday evening. The speaker was Jim McKendrick from America. The four men all agreed to come to our house for supper. While at our home, I took the opportunity to offer them some much-needed clothing (which was gratefully received). I had been given some good quality clothing for that very purpose by the family of a dear brother in the Lord who had recently died. As it was early in the New Year, they also took back to the ship some left-over Christmas chocolates for their mates!

I returned to the ship later the following week, to see if the ship was still in dock, and discovered that the departure of the ship had been delayed by engine trouble. That same week, I was admitted to hospital and was there for almost a week, returning home on Sunday afternoon. My return home coincided with a phone call from the Chief Officer of the ship. He wanted to come to our Gospel Service, he said, and some crew members wanted to come too! I quickly enlisted the help of two of our church members, brother Bert Gamble and brother Robert Laird, who very kindly took their cars to the docks to collect the seamen. Although just out of hospital, I decided to go too – to guide them to where the ship was berthed. The speaker that night was Dr. Jonathan Hannay, who explained with warmth and insight the meaning of the Christian faith. Altogether seven seamen came to our church that night – and they returned to their ship happy!

Japan's Big Ship

In all my time at the docks in Glasgow, the largest ship I ever encountered was a Japanese ship of enormous bulk and tonnage. It was just making its way in to its berth as I was leaving the docks about six o'clock one Sunday afternoon. I was visiting the docks in the hope of persuading some seamen to come with me to the gospel service in my church, Bethesda Hall. There was one ship already in the dock - a Norwegian ship, about to discharge a load of cement. I decided to delay boarding this ship. I usually avoid boarding ships when they are unloading cement because of the unhealthy, thick, white dust that swirls around as they unload. The dust often covered my car – so I thought breathing-in the dust could just as easily cover my lungs!

But, just before leaving the dock, I took one last glance down river, and it was then I noticed the big ship coming slowly round the last bend. The river at this point has many dangerous bends which ships have to navigate around - often with difficulty. I scanned the ship through my binoculars (a gift from the captain of one of the ships I had been on previously; they were German-made binoculars dating from before WW1 (1914-18) - and very effective). I watched as this large ship, slowly made its way round the final bend. It was going so slowly you could hardly see it move, and it had four tugs guiding it: two at the front and two at the back. At that pace, I realised that if I waited until the ship had berthed, and lowered the gangway, I would be late for the gospel meeting. Focusing my binoculars again, I noticed the crew consisted of slightly-built men with light brown skin. I surmised that they were Filipinos or men from Thailand.

When I returned the next day to visit the ship, I discovered to my surprise that the crew were from Japan. I was happy about this as I was interested in Japan, having just finished reading a book about Japan by a friend from Northern Ireland who had served with his wife and four children as a missionary in that country for many years, beginning in 1946. His name was Leonard Mullen and he came from the seaside town of Carnlough on the Antrim Coast. Before Len Mullen left Northern Ireland for Japan in 1946, many people tried to put him off going, saying that it was too close to the end of WW2 to visit an "enemy" country. Memories were still vivid of Japan's wartime exploits. But Leonard was not deterred.

My wife and I spent our summer holidays in Leonard's home town of Carnlough for many years and enjoyed the place immensely. We always stayed at Bethany Christian Guest House, owned by James and Mary Aiken, and it was a joy to join the Open Air Meetings at the Harbour in Carnlough in mid-July. The "open airs" were often followed by supper in Len Mullen's bungalow in the Largy Road or at James and Mary Aiken's Guest House.

Leonard's devotional life was very much in evidence. His preaching was original and typical of his gentle spirit. He wrote many choruses and hymns from the Bible set to his own tunes. Leonard loved to write about Carnlough too:

> *There is a place I dream of,*
> *A place I love the most,*
> *It bears the name of Carnlough,*
> *Along the Antrim Coast.*
>
> *It's curtained by the mountains*
> *And hemmed-in by the sea,*
> *There's not a spot in all the world*
> *That means so much to me.*

It clusters round the harbour
And sweeps along the bay,
But the most alluring place of all
Is out the Largy way.

But Carnlough needs the gospel,
Which God's forgiveness brings,
For these kind folks are careless
About eternal things.

There I would serve my fellows,
As God gives me the grace,
To tell of how He gave His Son
For folks in that dear place.

Leonard Mullen was called by God to Japan and he remained there with his family for many years teaching the Japanese people the gospel message of God's love and forgiveness. He was greatly loved by the Japanese people and, when Leonard and his family returned home, many Japanese people found their way to Carnlough to visit him.

My visit to the Japanese ship was a great success, spurred on as I was by memories of dear Leonard Mullen.

When I was twelve years old, a special preacher from Northern Ireland came to Plantation Gospel Hall to preach the gospel. He was a big stout man with a very loud speaking voice - and he sang even louder. His preaching engagement lasted for a good number of weeks. What I did not like about him was that, at the end of the gospel service, he would stand at the door as the people were leaving in order to shake hands with them. Nothing wrong with that, but I was a very shy boy, and did not like being singled out for special attention. He would shake my hand and say, "Well, boy, are you saved?" in his loud voice. I was too shy to answer. Worse was to come. Having enquired my name beforehand, he shook my hand as usual as I was going out the door and said, in a louder voice than ever (or so I imagined) so that all the waiting people would hear, "Well, Sammy, are you not saved yet?" He shook my hand and would not leave go! I did not answer and walked on, blushing furiously. He meant well, I suppose, but I thought he was bullying me to give a positive answer. It was shortly afterwards, when he had gone back to Ireland, that I trusted Jesus as Lord and Saviour at the end of a gospel service in a quiet and simple way. I had been troubled in my heart about the return of the Lord Jesus and was determined to settle this very important matter once and for all.

Whenever I have given my testimony, since that evening 75 years ago, I have quoted the words of the old gospel hymn:

> *I need no other argument,*
> *I need no other plea,*
> *It is enough that Jesus died,*
> *And that He died for me.*

Merkland's Wharf

Merkland's Wharf in Glasgow is not in use now. I remember it well as the place where cattle were unloaded from the old Burns & Laird line ships - such as the Laird's Rose, the Laird's Glen and the Laird's Loch. I was only a boy and the unloading of cattle which had come from the farms in Northern Ireland was of great interest to me. I was able to observe this at first hand when I was on board the Laird's Rose, returning to my tenement home in Glasgow after spending my summer holidays at my grandfather's farm in Co. Tyrone.

I leaned over the deck-rail at about six o'clock in the morning as the Laird's Rose slowly nosed her way towards Merkland's Wharf. On the overnight journey from Londonderry to Glasgow, as I lay trying to sleep on deck, I could hear the cattle lowing in the holds below. I felt sorry for them crammed into such a confined space. A short few hours before they had been enjoying the fresh green grass and the freedom of the Irish fields!

After we had docked at Merkland's Wharf, a special extra-wide gangway was fixed to the ship and the hold doors were opened on the ship's side. The drovers who travelled with the cattle carried long sticks to control the cattle, and to guide them into the large cattle trucks waiting on the quayside. They bellowed at the tops of their voices as the cattle reluctantly began to move down the wide gangway.

From the passenger deck, I watched as the poor cattle wandered slowly towards the trucks, amidst the shouts and the beatings of the sticks on their backs, probably frightened almost out of their lives. Sometimes some of the cattle would come to a standstill and refuse to move or go any further despite the wielding of the sticks. The drovers would then twist their tails until they moved – although I could hardly look as I thought it was cruel. But the shouting and the din and the bustle was all very exciting for me, as a young boy, and part of my holiday too, as I returned to Glasgow from my grandfather's farm. His farm, called Tyrkernaghan, was beautifully situated among the heather and the hills, close to the shores of Moorlough. The memory of it has lasted all my life-long. And now, as I engage in the Lord's work as Port Missionary to Glasgow Docks, I tell seamen from all over the world of the God who loves them and of Jesus Christ, who died to be their Saviour.

Sometimes, when I am on a big ship, right on the topmost deck, I think I can catch a glimpse of Merkland's Wharf, now closed, and the memories come flooding back.

Sea Clyde

This ship had a Scottish name – but an all-Russian crew! The man on watch met me at the top of the gangway. He told me to follow him and took me up to the Captain's cabin. This does not often happen, as ships' Captains are usually busy when the ship is in port and do not like to be interrupted - but this Captain welcomed me and gave me coffee. He then took me to the mess room and remained for a short time. The other seamen were there and I put some Christian literature on the table, including a supply of New Testaments. I also gave them hand-knitted woolly hats. The Captain then left the mess room to return to his work.

Then a fine young man came in. He was the Chief Officer and was interested to talk about Christian matters. He spoke good English. We had a good talk together. I told him about the Emmaus Courses. He told me that the ship would be leaving the next day. He and a few others came to the car when I was leaving and I gave them some good quality clothing I had received from my friend Norman Gourley. One was a good sheepskin coat which the Chief Officer gratefully received. On my way home, I thought again about the Emmaus Courses I had told the Chief Officer about and, as the ship was leaving the next day, I decided to return to the ship with a number of courses the next morning for the Chief Officer. I did this and found him in his cabin. He was glad to get the Emmaus Courses - and so I left a happy Chief Officer. I told him to return his Course to me when he had completed it and I would send him a Certificate as well as the next course. We should pray for this fine man.

M/V Milac Star

I boarded this ship in the month of March. I gave the last few Christian calendars I had left for that year, out of 600 I had purchased in the previous November, to six Filipinos in the crew. There was a veteran seaman on this ship with whom I had a good chat. He was very happy with the woolly hat and diary I had given him. He took me to his cabin to show me a large sailing ship model he was building in his spare time. He said it would take at least another six months to finish it. His cabin was like a joiner's workshop. I invited him to come to our church to the gospel meeting on the forthcoming Sunday evening – but he would not promise. However, the six Filipinos were happy to come.

When Sunday came round, I collected the Filipino seamen and took them to church. Stephen Dodds of Newtongrange was the speaker. His presentation is always excellent. He speaks very clearly and slowly so that everyone, even those who are just learning the English language, can hear and understand.

Stephen has a window cleaners' business. Shortly after speaking at our church he was perched on one of his tall ladders when he over-balanced and fell to the ground. He broke several bones in the fall and was seriously injured. Happily, after many months, he made a good recovery. I believe he has returned to his old occupation: cleaning windows! There is truth in the old saying: "You can't keep a good man down" – especially when he is on the topmost rung of the ladder!

Nigg Bay

I met Jimmy, a Glasgow man, some years ago. He had just come back from Nigg Bay, a lonely outpost of land in the North of Scotland, where he had been employed in building the first oil rig to be built in Scotland.

It was a desolate place, but they could earn big money. They lived in huts. In their spare time, there was nothing to do and nowhere to go – so they played cards into all hours of the night; and then someone would be accused of cheating, which would be vehemently denied, and fights would break out. It was, Jimmy said, a dark nightmare of a life and he had to get out or it would have driven him crazy.

So he came back to his home in the Maryhill district of Glasgow. He was not long home when he received an invitation to come to the Mission Hall in Maryhill. Jimmy responded to this and became a regular attender. Then one evening, God saved him. He said it was like going from darkness into light. Jimmy says the words "to save" means "to rescue" and he knew God had saved him from a dark world of sin. He knew in his heart that he had a Saviour in Jesus, who would never forsake him, and a sure and certain hope of a home in Heaven. One day Jimmy visited an old friend who had also been a worker at Nigg Bay. Billy lived by himself – also in Maryhill. For some time, Jimmy had been trying to get Billy to come to the Mission Hall. One day, Jimmy had brought his dog with him on a visit to Billy's house. As they were talking, Billy asked the question, "What like will it be in Heaven, Jimmy?" Jimmy was not too sure how to answer this question. Just then there was a sudden scraping and scuffling at the door. "What was that?" said Billy looking round quickly. "I've not heard anything like that at my door before!" Jimmy laughed. "That's my dog that you hear! Because he has never been here with me before, he is seeking me out. He is getting worried. I did not want to bring him in to your house, so I told him to wait outside the door. He knows I am in here with you and he wants me to open the door and let him in."

Then Jimmy remembered about the famous painting by Holman Hunt of Jesus Christ standing outside a closed door. On the painting were the words of Christ Himself "Behold I stand at the door and knock. If anyone hears my voice and opens the door, I will come in to him, and eat with him, and he with Me." "You see, Billy," explained Jimmy, "Jesus is calling for you to open the door of your heart and let Him in, in the same manner as my dog is calling for me to open the door to him."

Billy thought about this for a while and then said "Open the door Jimmy and let him in!" But Jimmy replied, saying "No! No! Billy. You must open the door!" Billy looked thoughtful for a few moments, and a tear ran down his cheek, and he got up and opened the door.

Operation Hospital!

In the Spring of 2001, I changed my routine of visiting the docks in the early afternoon. In April of that year, my wife Wilma was admitted to the local hospital to await an operation for breast cancer – so, instead of going to the docks in the early afternoon, I left it until the early evening and visited the hospital, which is close to King George V Docks, on my way home. This fitted in well with hospital visiting hours.

When considering this change of routine I wondered if there would be any ships in the docks in the early evening as, nowadays, ships have a quick turnaround to avoid hefty dock dues – but I was pleased to find that there were always ships in dock when I drove through the security gates and into "dockland".

Wilma's operation went ahead and was followed by chemotherapy and radiotherapy. It was a stressful time - but we are grateful to God that the cancer has not returned.

The Lady Who Could Not Take
A Calendar

One cold Saturday morning, as I was on my way to the Glasgow Docks, I stopped at Govan Cross to give out some gospel calendars. Business was fairly brisk as most people like to receive a calendar, especially if it is free! A respectable-looking lady stopped and I handed her a calendar. I was about to have a little word with her about the calendar when she said to me, "Would you give me a couple of pounds? I am going for the subway and I am a bit short."

I was not too much taken aback by this request as I get quite a lot of this sort of thing as I stand in the streets with gospel literature - and it is not always easy to deal with. This lady was not a down-and-out. I looked at her thoughtfully, "If you are back here at the same time next Saturday, and if you have begun reading the Bible I gave you, starting at the book of John, we will see how we get on. Meantime, I will give you £1." "Thank you," she said, and quickly turned towards the subway. I moved away in the opposite direction.

There was no sign of this lady the following Saturday as I was giving out the last of the calendars for the forthcoming year – but then I saw another lady coming towards me and I offered her a calendar. For a moment I had thought it was the lady from the previous Saturday, but, no, it was not. This lady looked at the calendar and said "There are texts on it!" I said, "Yes - it is a Christian calendar." She took a step back. "I cannot take it." "Why not?" I asked, genuinely surprised. And in a low voice, the lady said, "I'm Jewish." Then she hesitated, and looked again at the calendar, and said again "No, I cannot take it." I said, "I understand." And she walked away towards the subway.

I felt sorry for this dear lady. I called to her "I will see you again." But I knew in my heart that I would not. Next time it was likely that she would avoid me and take a different route to save any embarrassment.

I have not seen either of these ladies again.

Surprised by the Ladies!

I am sometimes surprised by the presence of lady visitors on board ship - but some are not visitors at all, but genuine crew members!

Recently I met a man from Zimbabwe who introduced me to his daughter. He was a nice man and his daughter was nice too, and was interested enough to take a couple of Christian calendars. Another lady was introduced to me on an Indian ship as the Captain's wife. She was tall and very thin, and came from Calcutta.

I met quite a number of Russian ladies who worked on the Russian ships – mostly in the mess rooms. One young lady about twenty, called Marina, came to the gospel service.

A good number of American ladies appeared over the years and came to the gospel service. One, indeed, was a ship's captain. Another American lady had flown over when her husband's ship had docked in Glasgow specially to see him. She brought him to the gospel service and to our home. After a few days she returned to America.

Another lady on an Isle of Man ship was the Chief Officer and was dressed all in white. She was not too keen to let me on her ship and could not get rid of me quickly enough! I don't think she took any Christian literature. However, I managed to leave the ship all in one piece.

I met Miranda on an American ship. She came to the gospel

service and later came to our home for coffee. She was a wonderful young lady, friendly and adaptable. She loved the old gospel hymns and was very enthusiastic. She was the only girl out of a crew of 20.

Most crews on board ship consist only of men – but, occasionally, it is nice to be surprised by the presence of the ladies!

The Big Teddy Bear

It was the day after Christmas. I had been at the docks on Christmas morning, as was my usual way, with carrier bags full of goodies for the ships that were in dock on that special morning.

At once I saw a new ship, one that had not been in dock on Christmas morning, so I parked my car in front of the ship and raked in the boot of my car for something to give to the crew. I found a left-over box of chocolates – seamen all seem to like British-made chocolate – and I put it in a carrier bag along with a selection of woolly hats. I searched for the Christian literature I usually hand out to seamen and I put some reading material in the bag too - calendars, Seed Sowers' texts, New Testaments and tracts.

I boarded the ship without difficulty and found my way to the mess room where two of the crew were sitting at a table, pretty drunk. Amazingly, as it turned out, the seamen were not from China, Russia, or the Philippines (as I would have expected) – one was from Ireland and the other was from Scotland! Although it was Sunday, I did not mention the service at our church, Bethesda Hall, in case they would want to come with me and, perhaps, disturb the meeting.

There was a large Christmas tree in the mess room festooned with decorations. One of the men decided to show me hospitality. "Have a drink, have a drink," he said, in a slurred voice. "Look!" I said, quickly changing the subject, "Have a chocolate!"

I had been on this ship before, so I was anxious to meet the

Captain. He was from Cork, a decent man who had visited our church when his ship had previously docked in Glasgow. I found him in the Officers' lounge along with a man from Ghana, his Chief Officer. He was pleased to see me. They would like to have come with me to the gospel service but they had arranged to visit a friend in Glasgow.

I later received a nice letter from the Captain, and the crew, thanking me for visiting the ship at Christmas-time. My visit had certainly made one man very happy – Alan the cook! I had promised Alan a large teddy bear.

My next-door neighbour had given it to me for a seaman's child. I went back the following day with the giant teddy bear. It looked new and was 3 feet high! I am sure it was bigger than some real bears! Alan was delighted with it and was sure his little girl would love it!

The two drunken seamen on board this ship gave me no trouble, but I had had trouble with drunken seamen before. They can be found on any ship and can come from all parts of the world. In this case, a few of the crew began by being belligerent – even occupying my car and refusing to get out - because of my refusal to take them to church drunk and incapable. But by God's good grace I was able to carefully calm them down by offering them T-shirts and woolly hats. In the end, they went away happy, not just by the alcohol they had consumed but by the gifts they had received – and I was able to make my escape!

The Woolly Hats of Auchlochan
- and many other places

When I began to visit the ships at Glasgow's King George V Docks I realised that I would need something to introduce myself by to the seamen! It was fine to tell them who I was, and what I was doing on their ship – but they would continue to stare at me unless they could be assured of my goodwill. I needed something to give them confidence in me and to reassure them that I was not a man come to exploit the poor seamen. I told them that I was the Seamen's Christian Visitor for Glasgow Docks, or the Port Missionary as I was sometimes called, and that I had Bibles and books to give them (all free!). I had also brought with me, I added, a supply of hand-knitted woolly hats to keep out the cold!

The story of the woolly hats began when I was invited to Auchlochan Retirement Village to speak to a group of ladies about my work for the Lord among the seamen. These ladies had heard "of a man called Sam" who visited the ships and they wanted to hear more about it. Auchlochan is situated about twenty miles from Glasgow.

Soon after my visit, the Auchlochan Knitting Group (for so it came to be called) began knitting woolly hats in all shapes and sizes, in bright rainbow colours, and in sober navy blue and black. Over the years, they have knitted hundreds of hats. And what a blessing these hats have been to the seamen when they faced the fierce winds and freezing rain and sleet of the oceans of the world. Mrs. Chrissie Simmonds, the gentle spokesperson of the group, greatly encouraged me and remembered me before the Lord in prayer. Several other ladies in Auchlochan knitted woolly hats too. Mrs. Sophia Waugh's lovely hand-knitted hats were delivered straight to me by her daughter, Elizabeth Gamble. Sometimes, too, when my wife and I returned to our house after being out shopping, we would find a huge bag of woolly hats sitting on the doorstep! We knew then that Mrs. Helen McDermott had called!

Beautifully knitted woolly hats by the score, also came from Wishaw Ebenezer Missionary Group, via Peter Hinshelwood and his wife Ruth.

Whenever I boarded a ship, and distributed my supply of woolly hats, I found the seamen friendly and open to the story of God's love through the Lord Jesus Christ. Thus the hand-knitted woolly hats were a great blessing spiritually – as well as a warm comforter on a wintry day on the Atlantic!

A Poem About Sunday School

When I was just a little boy, my Mother said to me,
"It's time you went to Sunday School". I said, "I'm far too wee."
"You're not too wee!" she said to me, "A great big boy like you!
You're nearly five, so off you go and learn things good and true!"

For years I went each Sunday, with my Bible in my hand,
I learned to love the stories that are told in every land,
Of David and Goliath and mighty Samson too,
And girls like Ruth and Esther – the Lord's work they did do.

I heard, too, of Zaccaeus, who climbed a great big tree;
There was no other way for him - his Lord he had to see.
And of Daniel in the lions' den, who prayed to God for aid,
And God just shut the lions' mouths – and the people were amazed.

But best of all was Jesus, He came to heal and save,
He paved the way to God for us if we will but believe,
Our Saviour suffered on the cross, nailed up between two thieves,
And all who put their trust in Him eternal life receive.

It made me sad whene'er He died on a hill called Calvary,
They took His body from the cross and in the grave he lay;
It was a thing most wonderful, such love – how could it be?
That God's own Son should come from Heaven to die for you and me.

And then He rose triumphantly; He came back from the dead,
And at the age of 13 years "I'll trust you, Lord," I said –
In a wee hall in Plantation, in dear old Glasgow town.
And since that day so long ago, He's never let me down.

A Poem About Sunday School

I never shall forget the things I learned at Sunday School,
They kept me strong and faithful when the devil tried to rule;
Across the sea toward Suez to India's sun-scorched land,
I recalled the hymns of Sunday School and knew He held my hand.

I thank my God for the Sunday School - I'm glad I didn't miss
The chance to give my life to God – a life that's really His.
Why don't you also take that step - He'll stay right to the end,
And praise and worship our great God, our Saviour and our Friend.

Sam Laughlin
1970

INVITATION TO CHURCH

PORT MISSIONARY, MR. SAM,
INVITES SEAMEN TO CHURCH SERVICE

WILL CALL THIS SUNDAY AT 6.00 p.m. (18.00 HOURS)

AFTERWARDS AT MR. SAM'S HOUSE FOR TEA

ALL WELCOME

Fisher of Men at Glasgow Docks